CLASSIC GUITARS

of the '50s

CHARLES ALEXANDER • TONY BACON • DAVE BURRLUCK

WALTER CARTER • PAUL DAY • ANDRE DUCHOSSOIR

THOMAS GOLDSMITH • STAN JAY & LARRY WEXER

JOHN MORRISH • HIROYUKI NOGUCHI • RIKKY ROOKSBY

PAUL TRYNKA • TOM WHEELER • MICHAEL WRIGHT

CLASSIC GUITARS OF THE FIFTIES

MILLER FREEMAN BOOKS
FIRST AMERICAN EDITION 1996

PUBLISHED IN THE UK BY BALAFON BOOKS, AN IMPRINT OF OUTLINE PRESS LTD.
115J CLEVELAND STREET, LONDON W1P 5PN, ENGLAND.

PUBLISHED IN THE UNITED STATES BY MILLER FREEMAN BOOKS
600 HARRISON STREET, SAN FRANCISCO, CA 94107
PUBLISHERS OF 'GUITAR PLAYER' AND 'BASS PLAYER' MAGAZINES
MILLER FREEMAN, INC. IS A UNITED NEWS AND MEDIA COMPANY

ISBN 0-87930-427-8
LIBRARY OF CONGRESS CATALOG NUMBER 96-84580

PRINTED IN HONG KONG

CREATIVE DIRECTOR: NIGEL OSBORNE
DESIGN: SALLY STOCKWELL
PHOTOGRAPHY: MIKI SLINGSBY
ILLUSTRATIONS: MARION APPLETON
EDITOR: TONY BACON

TYPESETTING BY KEVIN DODD & MICHAEL CUSHING AT TYPE TECHNIQUE, LONDON W1
PRINT & ORIGINATION BY REGENT PUBLISHING SERVICES

96 97 98 99 00 5 4 3 2 1

CONTENTS

The 1950s created the teenager; the teenager demanded pop music; and pop music's shiniest icon was the electric guitar. This book magnifies the links in that chain, and will plug you in to a decade of astonishing contrasts, blinding invention and great, great music.

The world was changing rapidly in the 1950s. World War II had ground to a bloody halt in 1945. It had shaken some countries to bits, reduced others to bankruptcy, given renewed confidence to a lucky few. Despite the ruins and the indelible marks of suffering, as the 1940s gave way to the 1950s people were determined to enjoy themselves at last, to celebrate their survival and continuing existence. One obvious way was through music.

Sex was popular too. "The abnormally high birth rate since 1940," said a US financial report of 1950, "has continued through 1949 and has resulted in about 33 million births which soon will have an important influence on school facilities, on housing and on food requirements." And, more crucially perhaps, on new trends in leisure and entertainment. "The great social revolution of the last 15 years," wrote Colin MacInnes in 1958, "[may be] the one that's given teenagers economic power… for let's not forget their 'spending money' does not go on traditional necessities, but on the kinds of luxuries that modify the social pattern."

The stage was set for change: many kids who grew up in the war were tougher and more independent than those who had gone before. They were ready for anything – and they wanted more. The new teenagers of the 1950s – only later would they be called 'Baby Boomers' – were greater in numbers than ever before compared to the overall population. Crucially, they had money in their pockets and a new-found freedom in which to spend it, more or less as they chose. A survey of American teenagers' spending habits in 1958 revealed that they represented a buying power of no less than $9 billion. And more often than not, at the top of their wish list was the latest rock'n'roll record.

Businessmen were not slow to appreciate the link between music listening and music making. The Harmony guitar company, for example, teamed up with Decca Records in 1955 for their Dance-O-Rama promotion where, as they described it, "Guitar players will be inspired to buy records and record fans will be encouraged to buy the instrument they like to hear."

Not only did the 1950s host the birth of rock'n'roll, but the new music led inevitably to a concentration on the guitar as one of the prime instruments at the heart of this musical revolution, aimed at and often created by teenagers (or, at least, by teenagers at heart). The United States was the site of this revolutionary melting pot, and the newly created mixtures were whisked rapidly around the world.

And yet these were far from idyllic times. Always close to the headlines in the 1950s was the potential peril inherent in atomic or nuclear power. It seemed only a matter of time before someone would lift the lid of this Pandora's box and finish everyone off for good. The threat of The Bomb was omnipresent – maybe it could

resolve the Korean War, or sort out Suez? After all, it had finished a much bigger war just years earlier. Nuclear fallout shelters sprang up as a rather inappropriate defense. And in the quickly developing climate of the cold war, no one in the West had much doubt as to who would be hurling the bombs at them.

Reactions to the Communist Threat of the dastardly Russians ranged from the typically unimaginative politician (Harry Truman: "Our lives, our nation, all the things we believe in, are in great danger, and this danger has been created by the rulers of the Soviet Union") to the more subtle innuendo of the movie house, where the sci-fi-Shakespeare of Forbidden Planet starred an unstoppable terror that roamed a doomed world, killing everyone.

As if all this wasn't enough, you just couldn't trust anyone – spies were everywhere. No matter: J Edgar Hoover and the FBI would be the protectors of every true US citizen. Spy fever reached its terrifying climax when American couple Julius and Ethel Rosenberg, found guilty of running a nuclear-espionage ring that passed information to the USSR, were executed by electric chair in 1953 – the first Americans ever sentenced to death for spying, in war or peacetime.

For many people living through the period, the 1950s were a peculiar mix. There were great leaps being made in science and technology, some of which were distant and hard to grasp, like rockets blasting into space, while others such as transistor radios or stereo records were closer to home and easy to appreciate. But underpinning all the innovation was a general unease, a feeling that the world was an unruly place that was spinning out of control. As Jack Kerouac, founder of the so-called Beat Generation, had one of the characters say in On The Road: "I had nothing to offer anybody except my own confusion."

America had the new music, at least for the time being, and so America had the guitars. Meanwhile, Europe had it bad. In Britain, for example, there was one word that came up again and again to describe the mood. Austerity. Post-war austerity. Rationing lasted well into the 1950s, bomb sites were everywhere, grayness and gloom prevailed, and thanks to a cash-strapped government the importing of musical instruments and gramophone records "from the dollar areas" was banned from 1951 to 1959. Rock'n'roll inventiveness necessarily lagged behind the American model, which was streaking ahead with tailfins glinting. Even politician Harold Macmillan's famous line, "You've never had it so good," delivered in 1957 when prospects had brightened, was taken from a US election slogan of five years earlier.

Relatively speaking, the United States had finished the 1940s without the crippling expense and psychological fallout that so many European countries had suffered as a result of World War II. Of course, there were some financial burdens – and the US musical instrument industry, at least, endured a recession from the late 1940s until about 1952. One can tell that there must have been a recession, because the contemporary press was flecked with articles insisting that there was no recession.

In fact the guitar started the 1950s at a disadvantage. A craze for the ukulele had begun at the end of the 1940s in the US, where over three million of the irritating little things were sold up to 1953. Fashion hounds everywhere forced their fingers into cramped chord shapes. The lowly ukulele was even elevated in 1950 to the status of an instrument recognized by the musicians' union in the New York area.

The accordion, too, was on the crest of a popular wave, buoyed up by bandleader and accordionist Lawrence Welk. His proto-MOR 'champagne music' was alone enough to make any self-respecting teenager seek musical alternatives. In jazz and early rock'n'roll it was the saxophone which dominated the instrumental frontline, and only in country, blues and Les Paul's multi-layered chart hits did the guitar start the decade with any kind of musical stronghold.

But by 1954 the guitar's fortunes were changing. A report by the American Music Conference in that year, estimating the number of people playing musical instruments in the US, put the guitar at 1.7 million, ukulele at 1.6 million and accordion at 950,000. The sax was lumped in with 'others' at 975,000.

Two years later, the dramatic rise of rock'n'roll underlined the guitar's versatility and fundamental simplicity, nudging the instrument to a peak of popularity. Charles Rubovits of the Harmony guitar company of Chicago seized on the positive signs when he wrote in a guitar industry report of 1956: "More people have the growing desire to do things themselves rather than be spectators; more people have more leisure time; more people are more easily exposed to music through television, creating a desire for self-expression; and more people have and will have more money to buy the things they want. Desire for fame and fortune is another motivating influence working in our behalf. Although we know the heights are reached by only a few, those attempting to gain this goal are many, proving this sales factor to be a reality."

Sidney Katz, president of the other big Chicago-based guitar manufacturer, Kay, told a trade gathering a few years later to overlook their own musical prejudices and chase the teenagers' dollars. "No matter how you feel about rock'n'roll and Elvis Presley," he said, "for business they have been great, and guitar sales have been rising steadily as a result. People are getting tired of sitting in front of a television set; they want to get together and entertain themselves – and there's no better instrument than a guitar for building a convivial atmosphere," Katz concluded. No doubt he had stressed exactly what his audience of businessmen wanted to hear: that big guitar sales would bring the American family closer together, singing wholesome songs together around the hearth. None of that rock'n'roll rubbish, that's for sure.

Reactions among parents and the establishment of the 1950s to Elvis and his brand of guitar-based jungle music ranged from the outraged to the morally indignant. "Rock'n'roll is the most brutal, ugly, vicious form of expression," Frank Sinatra told the New York Post in 1957, describing it colorfully as "the martial music

of every delinquent on the face of the earth." A vicar in England told the Daily Mirror that the effect of rock'n'roll on youngsters was "to turn them into devil worshippers; to stimulate self-expression through sex; to provoke lawlessness, impair nervous stability and destroy the sanctity of marriage." With that kind of manifesto, most teenagers merely wanted to know where to sign up.

Musical snobbery was rife, too. Steve Race, a British big-band pianist – and Light Music Advisor to the ATV television company – wrote in Melody Maker in 1956: "After Presley, just about anything can happen. Intonation, tone, intelligibility, musicianship, taste, subtlety – even the decent limits of guitar amplification – no longer matter. I fear for the future of a music industry which allows itself to cater for one demented age-group, to the exclusion of the masses who still want to hear a tuneful song, tunefully sung." It's a pity that Race didn't copyright that last bit, because it's been used ever since by every generation who can't help but criticize their kids' worthless music.

Jazzmen of the 1950s, too, were horrified by the inept noise and artless rhythms of the new music. Leading jazz guitarist Barney Kessel, used to his modestly amplified hollow-body electric guitar, but as a sessionman necessarily responsive to new sonic requirements, told a reporter in 1956: "I had to buy a special 'ultra toppy' guitar to get that horrible electric guitar sound that the cowboys and the rock'n'rollers want." And that same year a writer to the letters page in the jazz musician's chief magazine, Down Beat, was clearly affronted. "The epitome of this musical suicide is reached by persons of the ilk of Elvis Presley, who seems to have a talent for sneering, jumping up and down, crossing his legs, standing on his head, playing down to his audience – in fact, a talent for everything but music. What makes it worse is the fact that this guy is making out so well while more talented and deserving artists pick up the crumbs."

During the pages that follow, we'll analyze the decade's guitars and place them in the context of the music of the time. The guitars themselves, photographed to reveal every detail, provide the chronological order of the book, while around and about them a team of the world's top guitar writers bring their expertise to bear on the key elements in the story of the guitar-laden 1950s.

We see Chet Atkins at work on his pop-country hybrid and Les Paul constructing his New Sound, widening the popularity and appeal of the electric guitar; marvel at Tal Farlow reshaping the boundaries of jazz guitar playing; we hear the low-down twang of Duane Eddy's hit records; watch Scotty Moore at work with Elvis Presley, and Frank Beecher behind Bill Haley; investigate everything from the black R&B of Chuck Berry to the white pop of Buddy Holly; and examine Stratocasters and Explorers, Duo-Trons and Byrdlands, Emperors and Clubs and Switchmasters. Classic Guitars Of The Fifties for the first time explains how the electric guitar grew up and established itself during ten mesmerizing years. This book tells it like it was. ■ TONY BACON

7

△ EPIPHONE ZEPHYR EMPEROR REGENT
Also known as Zephyr Emperor Varitone
Produced 1950-1958; this example 1954

A startling mix of old and new, this traditionally styled hollow-body electric boasted three pickups, a panel of six tone-modifying switches, and a laminated maple top.

CONSTRUCTION

Almost all of the constructional concepts for the solidbody and semi-solid electric guitar were established in the 1950s, and more advances were made in those ten short years than in the two decades that followed.

Although numerous electric guitars existed before the 1950s, these were primarily hollow-body types (similar to the Epiphone shown here) or 'Hawaiian' lap steels. By combining the playing position of an electric 'Spanish'

hollow-body guitar with the solidity of a lap steel Leo Fender created what were as far as most musicians were concerned the world's first solidbody electric guitars, the Esquire and the Broadcaster. First produced in 1950 (and with the Broadcaster soon renamed Telecaster) these instruments laid the foundation and created the benchmark for factory-produced solidbody electric guitars.

Apart from the obvious solid body, it is Fender's bolt-on neck which has become the key constructional feature that

still allows instruments to be built in a cost-effective manner today. Initially the feature was instigated as a safeguard against component failure: a bolt-on neck was far easier to replace than the traditional glued-in or 'set' type favored by older guitar companies such as Gibson. Quite simply, Fender's bolt-on neck made electric guitar manufacturing easier and more economic.

Both Fender and Gibson were factory-production manufacturers. Leo Fender didn't hand-build his

CONSTRUCTION *by Dave Burrluck*

Change was constantly in the air during the 1950s as electric guitar makers responded to new musical trends where musicians demanded louder guitars. With the solidbody electric guitar it was an instrument manufacturer, Leo Fender, who introduced guitarists to a radical new idea. At first many traditional makers derided the apparently simple bolt-together instrument, but by the end of the decade almost every company offered a solidbody.

NEW IDEAS came from makers of hollow-body electric guitars as well as solidbody designers during the 1950s. In this 1950 ad (below) Epiphone stresses its use "for the first time" of a six-button "color tone" system.

instruments; nor did Ted McCarty at Gibson. From its birth, the solidbody electric guitar was a production item, something that had to be manufactured quickly and cost-effectively. The Broadcaster was designed as such from the start, and Fender, unencumbered by the heritage of traditional guitar making, revolutionized guitar production.

Bolt-on necks could be entirely finished, lacquered and stockpiled before fitting to a body. The guitar was 'created' simply by joining the two parts – body and neck – with four machine screws. Without the traditional angled-back headstock, timber usage was more economic, and there was no additional fingerboard material because Fender's neck was made of one piece of wood, save for a small fillet of contrasting timber installed from the rear.

When Gibson introduced the Les Paul 'gold-top' model in 1952 it bore little resemblance to Fender's Telecaster. Yes, both were single-cutaway, solidbody, twin-pickup

guitars... but there the similarity ended. In fact the two guitars could not have been more different. Where the Telecaster could be considered as a rather crude 'plank', the Les Paul dragged Gibson's decades-old archtop heritage into modern solidbody design. Gibson used their customary glued-in neck joint with a small, traditional 'heel', in marked contrast to the crude but wonderfully effective bolt-on neck and angular heel that Fender employed for their Telecaster.

The raw materials too reflected the difference. Fender chose indigenous woods such as lightweight ash for bodies, maple for necks. For their Les Paul, Gibson looked further afield to Central and South America for high grade mahogany for the neck and body and to Brazil for the rosewood fingerboard (plus maple for the carved top 'cap').

Whether the timbers were chosen for their structural and sonic properties, for their appearance, or simply for

HEADSTOCK (below) The beautiful and distinctive floral inlay design was used by Epiphone for many years.

INLAYS (above) This stylish design that contrasts creamy pearl and green abalone is a hallmark of Epiphone guitars.

THE EARLIEST electric guitars were produced in the 1930s. Rickenbacker's lap steel 'Frying Pan' prototype of 1931 was the first guitar to feature an electro-magnetic pickup, and as such was the basis for virtually all modern electric guitars. 'Spanish' type electrics also began to appear in the 1930s, made by companies such as National, Epiphone and Gibson. Rickenbacker's small Bakelite guitars of 1935 were among the first solidbody electrics, while in the 1940s Les Paul modified an Epiphone guitar to make his one-off electric 'Log', an early solidbody type instrument. Around 1947 engineer Paul Bigsby and musician Merle Travis collaborated on a guitar that looked closer to the idea of a modern solidbody electric than anything that had been made before, and Fender's Broadcaster (right) came on to the market in 1950.

FENDER made guitar building simple and cheap with the bolt-together Broadcaster.

Off the record

George Barnes

and his Gibson

BODIES of most 1950s Gibson hollow-body electrics had this 'rounded' cutaway (above); it became 'pointed' during 1960.

DISTINCTIVE touches on the Super 400CES fingerboard include the split-block inlays (above) and 'pointed' end (left).

THE SUPER 400's characteristic pickguard of 'marbleized' tortoiseshell (above) was created by a special plastic overlay.

double offset cutaway horns, three pickups, an advanced vibrato and that contoured body. Its design took Fender's crucial component-based production method a stage further – the Stratocaster's pickguard/pickup assembly was one separate part, just like the neck, and the body.

Viewed from a 1990s perspective the Telecaster, Les Paul and Stratocaster remain the key instruments of the 1950s, but the decade threw up many more constructional ideas that are important to the modern electric guitar. Rickenbacker is credited with the first production through-neck guitar, the 1956 Combo 400. By making the neck and central body section from one piece (or a laminate of longitudinal stripes) the vibration of the strings, and therefore the instrument's resulting sustain, is uninterrupted: there is no neck-to-body joint. However, some makers believe that the through-neck's central section limits low-end tonal response. Nonetheless the through-neck design has been featured by numerous companies, notably Gibson with its early 1960s Firebird design, and present-day Rickenbacker production. This expensive method is today popular with bass makers.

While the lion's share of attention has historically been focused on the Les Paul, Tele and Strat, Gibson's ES-335 was perhaps one of the most versatile instruments of the era, and has remained popular since its launch in 1958. In many ways the instrument exemplified Gibson's heritage more strongly than the company's Les Paul models. Gibson had established landmark hollow-body electrics with the launch in 1951 of the L-5CES and Super 400CES (as shown on these pages), and four years later the company experimented by marketing its first hollow 'Thinline' electric acoustics, the Byrdland and the ES-350T. In outline these models looked like typical Gibson archtop jazz guitars, but their bodies were much thinner, making for a less cumbersome instrument and one which to an extent reduced feedback when amplified.

In fact Gibson wanted a guitar with the tone and playability of a solidbody but the appearance and feel of a 'real' archtop guitar, and it was the ES-335 that supplied this combination. The new model boasted a fresh double-cutaway body shape constructed in traditional form with separate top, back and sides made from laminated maple,

▽ GIBSON SUPER 400CES
Produced 1951-current; this example February 1953

This was Gibson's top-of-the-line hollow-body electric guitar and, at nearly 3½in deep and 18in wide, the biggest. It was based on the existing Super 400C acoustic model, but with a slightly thicker top and stronger internal bracing to help prevent feedback. The P90 pickups of early models such as the example shown here were soon replaced by Alnico types and, later in the 1950s, by humbuckers.

PLAYERS *could raise or lower the Varitone tailpiece (above) to subtly alter tone by using an Allen key in the small hole on the unit.*

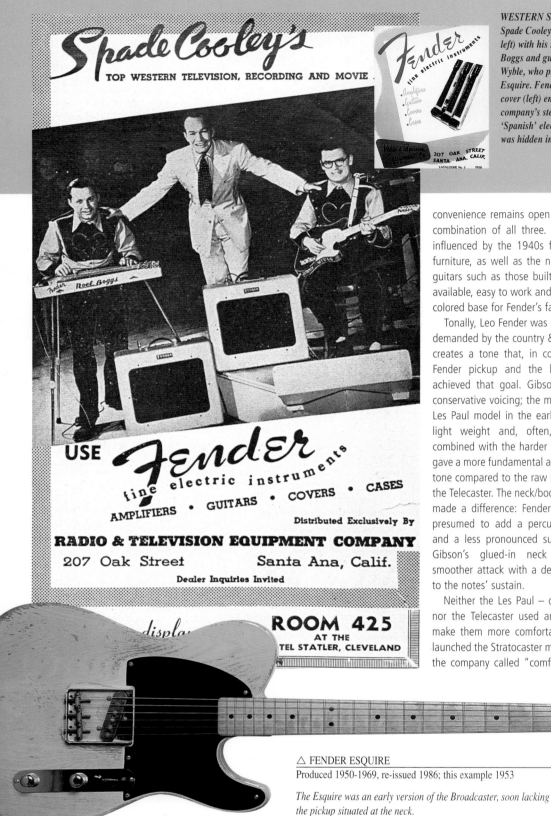

WESTERN SWING bandleader Spade Cooley is pictured (far left) with his steel player Noel Boggs and guitarist Jimmy Wyble, who plays an early Esquire. Fender's 1950 catalog cover (left) emphasizes the company's steel guitars; its new 'Spanish' electric, the Esquire, was hidden inside.

convenience remains open to question. It was probably a combination of all three. But Leo Fender was definitely influenced by the 1940s fashion for limed ash and oak furniture, as well as the natural 'blonde' look of archtop guitars such as those built by Epiphone. Ash was readily available, easy to work and, importantly, provided the light colored base for Fender's famous blonde finish.

Tonally, Leo Fender was looking for a clean, bright voice demanded by the country & Western market. The light ash creates a tone that, in combination with the single-coil Fender pickup and the bolt-on maple neck, certainly achieved that goal. Gibson, however, went for a more conservative voicing; the mahogany used by Gibson for its Les Paul model in the early 1950s was renowned for its light weight and, often, a stronger midrange that, combined with the harder maple 'cap', gave a more fundamental and articulate tone compared to the raw brashness of the Telecaster. The neck/body joints also made a difference: Fender's bolt-on is presumed to add a percussive attack and a less pronounced sustain, while Gibson's glued-in neck creates a smoother attack with a definite bloom to the notes' sustain.

Neither the Les Paul – despite its carved arched top – nor the Telecaster used any kind of body contouring to make them more comfortable to play, but when Fender launched the Stratocaster model in 1954 it came with what the company called "comfort contouring". The Strat had

△ FENDER ESQUIRE
Produced 1950-1969, re-issued 1986; this example 1953

The Esquire was an early version of the Broadcaster, soon lacking the pickup situated at the neck.

△ FENDER BROADCASTER
Produced 1950 only

Historically important as the world's first solidbody electric guitars produced in significant numbers, the Esquire and Broadcaster exemplified the simple, bolt-together construction used by Fender. Gradually during the 1950s Fender caused many rival manufacturers to evaluate and modify their production and marketing methods.

FENDER had to drop the name Broadcaster when another company proved prior use. At first 'Broadcaster' was simply clipped from the logo – nicknamed 'No-caster' models – but soon the new Telecaster name was in place.

THE KOREAN WAR starts in June when North Korean troops invade South Korea. The United Nations supports South Korea, China enters on the North Korean side, and the fighting escalates.

GEORGE BERNARD SHAW, Irish dramatist best known for 'Pygmalion', dies aged 94.

TELEVISION viewing matches radio listening in New York for the first time. In 1946 the US had seven TV stations; by the end of 1950 there are 107.

'THE THIRD MAN THEME' from the 1949 film (still and poster above) is released by zither player Anton Karas and sells four million copies during 1950, proving that catchy instrumental records can become big pop hits.

HIT RECORDS include Nat King Cole's 'Mona Lisa' which wins this year's Academy Award for best song. Patti Page's 'Tennessee Waltz' is a Number One smash, strongly outselling the rival version by Les Paul & Mary Ford.

DECCA issues the first LPs on to the UK market. Columbia in the US had issued the first $33^{1}/_{3}$ rpm 10in and 12in LPs in 1948, and RCA Victor the first 45rpm 7in EP records in 1949. LPs followed in Russia and France (1951), Germany (1952) and Spain and Denmark (1953).

MOST PROMINENT of all players of the Super 400CES in the 1950s was Scotty Moore (main picture, right) who used one during most of his work backing Elvis Presley in the studio and on stage. Moore signed the main photo and sent it to amplifier maker Ray Butts in 1956 to show Butts his EchoSonic amp in action.

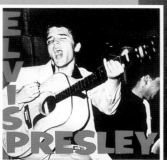

Ray - Here's The Amp →
MANY THANKS
Scotty Moore

BLOCK fingerboard markers and a 'torch' headstock inlay decorate the L-5CES (below).

△ GIBSON L-5SEC
Early examples of the L-5CES were labeled L-5SEC
Produced 1951-current; this example October 1951

Just before Gibson issued an electric version of its Super 400C guitar, the company combined elements of the acoustic L-5C and electric ES-5 models to create the L-5CES ('cutaway electric Spanish'). Like the Super 400CES, the L-5CES had a traditional carved spruce top, carved maple back, and maple sides.

A SPLIT-DIAMOND inlay on the headstock (right) instantly identifies a Gibson cutaway electric as a Super 400CES.

but with an added solid center block (much like Les Paul's original 'Log' design) stabilizing the top and back and giving the pickups, bridge and tailpiece a firm mounting. The design also meant that the neck joined the body at the 19th fret, so players had superb access to the upper frets.

Rickenbacker approached the 'semi-solid' guitar from a different angle. In the mid-1950s the company began hollowing out solidbody guitars, routing the body from the back to leave a solid center section, and with an additional back piece sealing the completed body. Rickenbacker did this to reduce body weight, and while at first it employed a semi-solid construction method on certain Combo models the company employed it most effectively on the Capri line. Launched in 1958, these models evolved into the soon-to-be-classic Rickenbackers such as the 330 and 360.

Gibson's post-war move to using laminated maple in guitar production had a direct effect on the long-term success of their ES-335. Using pressed, laminated maple (effectively maple ply) for a guitar's front and back reduced production costs but, even on earlier guitars such as the ES-350, contributed to a more fundamental tone with less of

△ D'ANGELICO EXCEL
Produced 1936-1964; this example 1952

Many players added pickups to acoustic guitars, commonly the DeArmond 'floating' units made by Rowe (see ad, right) which float free of the guitar's top and thus avoid interfering with the tonal integrity of the hollow body. With a guitar such as John D'Angelico's archtops, the idea was to amplify the guitar's inherent tone. But with the L-5CES and 400CES shown on these pages, Gibson built modified electric versions of acoustic guitars and began to seek a new and unique voice for the electric guitar.

De Armond
MICROPHONES FOR STRINGED INSTRUMENTS

...UNDISTORTED POWER VOLUME!

ROWE *Industries* 1702 WAYNE ST. TOLEDO 9, OHIO

DJ ALAN FREED begins his R&B radio program out of Cleveland, Ohio. Between now and 1954 he starts to call it a 'Moondog Rock 'n' Roll Party', and later claims he invented the term 'rock'n'roll'.

I LOVE LUCY, definitive 1950s TV sitcom, starts a ten year run with Lucille Ball as Lucy Ricardo and Desi Arnaz as Ricky the hard-pressed hubby.

WINSTON CHURCHILL (Conservative) replaces Clement Attlee (Labour) as Prime Minister in the UK, where post-war austerity fades a little as the Festival Of Britain is opened by King George VI in London.

J.D. SALINGER's 'Catcher In The Rye' is published. It is the story of Holden Caulfield, who sums up forever how oh-so-lonely it is to be an adolescent.

ARMISTICE negotiations, which become prolonged, open in Korea in July. Elsewhere, King Abdullah of Jordan is assassinated, and Libya becomes an independent state.

LES PAUL & Mary Ford achieve their first number one hit with 'How High The Moon', exemplifying Paul's multiple-layered recording techniques. The jazz magazine Down Beat seems surprised when Les Paul tops their readers' poll for Best Guitarist; runners-up votes are split between more traditional jazzers Billy Bauer, Tal Farlow and Chuck Wayne. In fact Paul will win the Down Beat poll for the next two years running.

LITTLE RICHARD's band, captured for 'The Girl Can't Help It' movie in 1956 and probably with Nathaniel Douglas on Telecaster, shows how Fender's guitars began to grow in popularity during the 1950s, reaching far beyond the company's initial market locally in California. Fender's solidbody guitars became a national sensation that other makers couldn't fail to notice.

A BLACK pickguard and fretted maple neck means an early Telecaster: a white guard was used from 1954 and a rosewood board from 1959.

LEO FENDER's full initials (standing for Clarence Leo) appear on his patent for the combined pickup and bridge unit, mounted into a simple metal plate, that is at the heart of the sound of the Telecaster. The strings pass through the body and are anchored at the back by six ferrules, giving solidity and sustain to the resulting sound, while the slanting pickup also enhances the guitar's natural treble tone.

THE ORIGINAL Fender ELECTRIC STANDARD GUITAR

1. Fine fast action.
2. True intonation.
3. Wide range tone effects.
4. Steel re-enforced adjustable neck.
5. Strings adjustable for length and height from fret board.
6. Pickups adjustable for tone response.
7. No feedback.
8. Last fret position accessable.
9. Modern design.
10. Single and double pickup models available.

All models c
beautiful top

Distributed B

RADIO & TELEVISION EQ

207 OAK STREET   SANTA ANA, CALIF.

Oct. 30, 1951   C. L. FENDER   2,573,254
COMBINATION BRIDGE AND PICKUP ASSEMBLY
FOR STRING INSTRUMENTS
Filed Jan. 13, 1950

FENDER began to advertise the newly named twin-pickup Telecaster along with the single-pickup Esquire during the early 1950s, and among the guitars' virtues listed in this 1952 ad (right) was 'no feedback'. This claim was directed at musicians who were used to the howls of feedback that would be heard from most hollow-body electric guitars when their amplifiers were turned up loud.

14

HANK THOMPSON and his BRAZOS VALLEY BOYS
Nation's No. 1 Western Recording Artist Recording exclusively on Capitol Records

Nation's No. 1 Western Swing Band.

PERSONAL MANAGEMENT—
JIM HALSEY

15½ S. WALKER, OKLAHOMA CITY, OKLA. PHONES—REGENT 6-8081, REGENT 6-0002

WESTERN SWING was a lively dance music that grew up in Texas dancehalls during the 1930s and 1940s, making notable and early use of electric guitars. Hank Thompson's Brazos Valley Boys created a commercial fusion of Western swing and honky tonk, hitting number one in 1952 with 'The Wild Side Of Life'. This 1953 lineup (left) includes Thompson with a personalized

Gibson/Bigsby, next to him the band's musical director Billy Gray on Gibson ES-5, and Bill Carson with a Fender Telecaster. Carson had obtained his Tele direct from Fender, partly paying for it by acting as a musical guinea pig for new products. Some of his misgivings over the Telecaster led to Fender's development of a new solidbody model, the Stratocaster, in 1954.

▽ FENDER TELECASTER
Produced 1951-current; this example 1953

The longest-running solidbody electric guitar model ever, the Telecaster is loved by a diverse range of players from all areas of music for its inherent simplicity and clean, cutting sound.

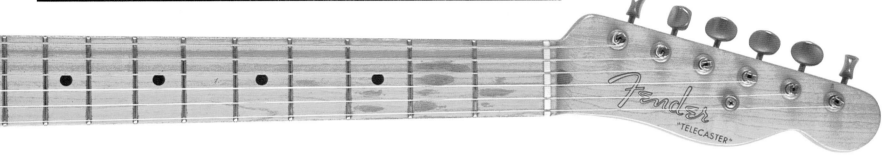

the acoustic-like harmonics contributed, for example, by a more traditional carved spruce top. Guitars with these laminated materials were preferred by many players for amplified work, and in the case of the ES-335 the laminated woods in combination with the guitar's semi-solid construction limited its acoustic properties anyway. When players in later generations used the ES-335 with high volume stage amplification its construction combated unwanted feedback, allowing controlled 'musical' feedback along with the 335's ever-present and distinctive woody tone. Like the Stratocaster, Telecaster and the humbucker-equipped Les Paul, the ES-335 proved to be a survivor of any changes in musical style and fashion.

This versatility is surely the key to the longevity both of guitar designs and construction

methods. Over time, the mark of a successful guitar is that it becomes successful in applications that were not envisaged by its designers. Guitars such as those made by Gretsch and Rickenbacker that tend towards the idiosyncratic have never achieved this iconic status, yet remain viable choices thanks to their individual sonic thumbprints. Fender's Jazzmaster of 1958 was intended to improve upon the Stratocaster, but it didn't. Despite the Jazzmaster's thicker sounds from wider single-coil pickups, a new vibrato design and a new body shape with an offset waist, plus some nifty electronics, it nonetheless lacked a Stratocaster's simplicity – which can often be at the root of a guitar's versatility.

One of Gibson's final flings in the 1950s was the development of its 'Modernistic' designs: the Explorer and

the Flying V. At the time, these guitars were seen and perhaps even intended as little more than a joke. But they proved within the space of a decade following their launch that the solidbody electric guitar could in fact adapt to any shape, could still sound good, and might even represent a fashion statement – perfect instruments, as it turned out, to propel the more overt musical styles such as heavy metal that were to emerge during the 1970s and 1980s.

Cynics in the 1990s sneer at contemporary guitar design, saying it's all been done before. And in fact there is little doubt that virtually all the solidbody and semi-solid guitar design classics were originated in the 1950s. But at the time few of the companies or individuals involved could have had any idea of the monster they'd created: the modern electric guitar. ■ DAVE BURRLUCK

MOST MAKERS had by the late 1940s followed Gibson's lead with a cutaway body (left).

△ VEGA E-300 DUO-TRON
Produced 1949-1956; this example 1951

Vega began in Boston around 1900 as a brass and banjo maker, by the 1930s adding guitars to the line. Electrics like the E-300 used traditional techniques, with "electric parts that in no way affect the body tone" thanks to a pickup fixed to the fingerboard and controls floating on the tailpiece. "So all the tonal advantages are in this instrument with or without amplifier," Vega

STAN KENTON (above) was an ambitious jazzman, prone to calling his band's 'Orchestras' and popular with audiences if

not critics. He is seen here during 1952 with his guitarist Ralph Blaze who plays a blonde Vega E-300 Duo-Tron.

THE GIBSON STORY *by André Duchossoir*

At the start of the 1950s Gibson was a successful US guitar-making company, some 45 years old, steeped in tradition... and faced with a dilemma. Should it continue to produce only the acoustic and 'electrified' acoustic guitars that had brought it such success, or should it also meddle with the new solidbody electric guitars that a small competitor was beginning to sell in increasing numbers? The answer came in the shape of the solidbody Les Paul model.

SOLIDBODY electric guitars immediately found favor during the 1950s with the new generation of urban bluesmen (such as Freddie King, seen below with Les Paul gold-top)

and honky tonk-style country & Western bands. Both were attracted by the penetrating tone, bright treble response and unusual sustaining power of the new instruments.

THE GIBSON STORY

Gibson's earliest attempts in the field of electric stringed instruments date from the mid 1920s, but it was not until 1935 that the company's first production model, a metal-bodied Hawaiian lap steel, was commercialized. In 1936 Gibson's hollow-body ES-150 'Spanish' electric was issued and became arguably the best-known electric guitar of the pre-war era thanks to its association with the pioneering electric jazz guitarist, Charlie Christian.

On the threshold of the 1950s Gibson produced some of the most popular electric guitars, but these various ES models, including the ES-295 shown here, were still largely rooted in pre-war concepts and patterned after traditional archtop acoustic designs. The most visible evolution since World War II had been the multiplication of pickups, culminating with a three-pickup layout on the ES-5 which premiered in 1949, but the hollow-body electric guitar — what might be termed the 'electrified' guitar — reached its apogee in 1951 with the inception of Gibson's Super

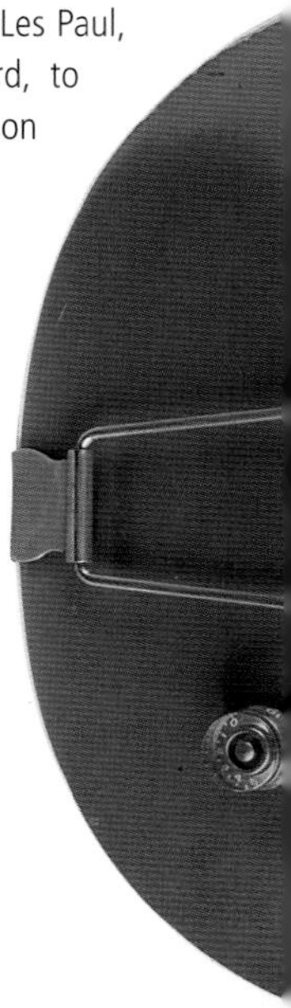

▽ GIBSON ES-295

Produced 1952-1958, re-issued 1990; this example June 1953

Until 1952 Gibson's guitars had come in traditional sunburst or natural finish. The gleaming gold of the hollow-body 295 was a shocking, eye-catching novelty that matched the visual impact of Gibson's new Les Paul solidbody model.

400CES and L-5CES. These superlative models, still considered by many as the finest jazz guitars, were essentially versions of the company's renowned acoustic counterparts, fitted with stronger bracing and twin pickups. But by the time these guitars were launched, a new challenge was already underway.

The success of the Fender Telecaster prompted Gibson to tread new paths where sounds and visual style mattered more than heritage and craftsmanship. Reluctantly but realistically, the company jumped on the bandwagon that Leo Fender had set rolling and came up with its own electric solidbody in 1952. To make up for a late start Gibson smartly enlisted the services of Les Paul, an accomplished guitarist and electronic wizard, to lend his name to the new guitar. Meanwhile, Gibson chief Ted McCarty and his associates developed a solidbody model that manifested everything the brand stood for, including a carved maple top that Fender could not duplicate.

The Les Paul model, painted with a gleaming gold top at Paul's request, was an instant success — in 1952/53 nearly 4000 were sold, more than 30 per cent of the combined production of all the archtop electrics made at that time at Gibson's Kalamazoo, Michigan, factory. After 1953 the sales of electrified archtops dropped, while Gibson forged ahead with a complete line of

WHITE single-coil P-90 pickups (left) on the original ES-295 were replaced by humbuckers in 1957.

THE ES-295 was launched some months after the gold-top Les Paul in 1952, and was effectively a gold finished ES-175 (see page 20/21) with a new tailpiece, white pickups and an attractively decorated white pickguard. But players of hollow-body guitars proved too conservative to be tempted by this shiny bauble, and the 295 did not last very long in the Gibson line.

GIBSON SALUTES LES PAUL

Congratulations, Les Paul, on winning the Down Beat Guitar Poll. We're proud of the interest in guitars fostered by your artistry, and we're proud, too, of the wonderful Gibsons now under construction for you and Mary. We are confident these fine instruments will inspire you to new feats of wizardry in your musical accomplishments.

GIBSON, INC., Kalamazoo, Michigan

LES PAUL & Mary Ford became huge stars in the early 1950s with hits like 'How High The Moon' that featured Paul's distinctive multi-layered recording techniques. He experimented with instruments too, and in the 1940s made his 'Log', an early semi-solidbody electric (seen with Paul and Ford on Ed Sullivan's TV show in 1951, left). Gibson eagerly signed the famous guitarist to endorse its new solidbody electric guitar in 1952, a relationship previewed in the company's ad, shown far left, where the Epiphone logo on the headstock of the 'Log' is carefully hidden.

Melody Maker
INCORPORATING 'RHYTHM'
Vol. 28. No. 961   FEBRUARY 16, 1952   EVERY FRIDAY - 6d.

DANCE MUSIC IS HUSHED AS NATION MOURNS

God Save the Queen

solidbody models bearing the Les Paul name: the top-of-the-line Custom, plus budget Junior, TV and Special.

As befits a high-end model, the black Les Paul Custom was endowed with Gibson's latest advances, such as the fully-adjustable Tune-o-matic bridge and a powerful Alnico pickup with adjustable magnets. The latter was a first effort towards improving Gibson's ubiquitous P90 single-coil pickup of early 1940s origin. But a real evolution would only materialize with the advent of the humbucking pickup, devised in 1955. The humbucker marked a watershed in guitar electronics and ultimately became an industry standard, the success of which relied on more than its ability to 'buck the hum', or cut noise. In 1957, both the regular Les Paul and the Custom were upgraded with the new pickup unit, used henceforth as the staple device on the company's senior models.

A request by famed country guitarists Billy Byrd and Hank Garland served as a catalyst for Gibson to design

KING GEORGE VI dies at Sandringham, England, while Princess Elizabeth is away on a Commonwealth tour. The new Queen takes up residence at Buckingham Palace three months later.

THE LES PAUL model (below) began to come off the Gibson production lines in 1952. It soon became clear that the guitar's trapeze tailpiece was inappropriate, and it was replaced during 1953 with a new unit (see overleaf).

WITH 'CRY', Johnnie Ray is the first white singer in the US to hit both pop and R&B charts, heralding the erosion of music's racial barriers.

ALL-GOLD versions of the Les Paul gold-top were made by Gibson during the 1950s.

△ GIBSON LES PAUL 'ALL-GOLD'
Special order 1952-1955; this example 1952.

While most Les Paul 'gold-top' models were just that, some were issued 'all-gold', with a gold body top, back and sides.

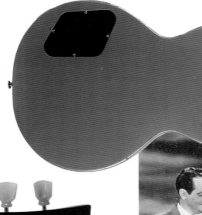

THE FIRST detonation of a hydrogen bomb – many times more powerful than an atom bomb – takes place at Eniwetok Atoll in the Pacific Ocean by the US. The first accident at a nuclear reactor occurs at Chalk River, Canada, without apparent casualties.

15th OLYMPIC GAMES are held at Helsinki, Finland.

MR. POTATO HEAD becomes the first children's toy to be advertised on television.

THE WORLD'S first fare-paying jet airliner passenger is Mr. A. Henshaw of Mablethorpe, England, who travels on a BOAC Comet on its first commercial flight from London to Johannesburg in May with 35 other passengers.

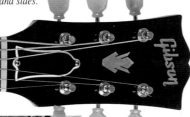

Gibson **Les Paul model**

It's a Sensation!

Designed by Les Paul—produced by Gibson—and enthusiastically approved by top guitarists everywhere. The Les Paul Model is a unique and exciting innovation in the fretted instrument field; you have to see and hear it to appreciate the wonderful features and unusual tone of this newest Gibson guitar. Write Dept. 107 for more information about it.

Gibson, Inc., Kalamazoo, Mich.

GIBSON president Ted McCarty (left) holds a special all-gold hollow-body made in 1951 at Les Paul's request for a hospitalized guitarist. It prompted Gibson's all-gold ES-295 production model.

LES PAUL promotes his new namesake model (right) in the gold-top's first ad, from 1952.

1953

TED McCARTY (right) was president of Gibson from 1950 to 1966, overseeing what many regard as the guitar company's golden period. A new one-story extension added in 1950 to the Kalamazoo factory (far right) marked Gibson's confidence as the decade began. The before and after shots (January 1950 above; July below) also show the original 1917 building.

its new thin-body electrics. Premiered in 1955, the Byrdland (named for its originators) and its sibling, the ES-350T, became the leading members of a family of electrics that would offer an alternative to the radical new solidbody designs without offending tradition-conscious archtop players. The two Thinline models looked like regular hollow-bodies, but were much more shallow, making them more manageable and less prone to feedback. Both the Byrdland and the ES-350T were also fitted with an extra-narrow short-scale neck to facilitate extended fingering and dazzling solo runs. Gibson had struck the right chord and the Byrdland was adopted by B.B. King among others, while a blonde 350T became the trademark of Chuck Berry. But blues and rock were not yet fashionable enough to warrant a photo of these two artists in Gibson's brochures.

Indeed, many dealers' reports had it that Gibson was perceived as too conservative and its products not as flashy or innovative as those of some other manufacturers. Irritated by these comments, Gibson boss Ted McCarty decided to bite the bullet when in late 1956 figures showed that sales of solidbody models had ceased to grow.

McCarty's response was a radical line of electrics appropriately dubbed the 'Modernistic Guitars'.

First sighted as prototypes in 1957 but available by 1958, the Flying V and the Explorer featured unusually angular, aggressive-looking shapes that instantly set them apart from anything else. In the late 1950s, though, their futuristic design was ahead of its time, and what now seems a bold initiative was a flop back then. A mere 81 Flying Vs and 19 Explorers were shipped in 1958, often to dealers who used them as a prop in their window displays. A third design called the Moderne never made it to the production line, and today its untraced prototypes are considered as the true Holy Grail of electric guitars. If anything, the Modernistic Guitars succeeded in shaking Gibson's stodgy image and in showing that a solidbody could take any shape at all — provided, of course, that customers were prepared to go along with the idea.

In 1958 Gibson suffered another blow, albeit less catastrophic, with its attempt to revive the slumping sales of the Les Paul model. To broaden the guitar's market appeal, its gold finish was replaced by a more traditional cherry sunburst, and it was soon renamed the Les Paul

Standard. Practically unnoticed in the late 1950s, this change of guise would eventually create the most sought-after solidbody guitar, acclaimed for its sound as much as its looks. Like the Modernistic Guitars, yesterday's failure would turn into tomorrow's treasure.

Despite the original fate of these influential designs, not everything turned sour in 1958 for Gibson, and the company scored at least two major hits. The double-cutaway body shape introduced to revamp the Les Paul Junior, TV and Special did exactly what it was intended to do: their combined sales doubled within a year.

The other success of 1958 was the ES-335T, which enabled Gibson to break new ground while maintaining its heritage that was rooted in f-hole guitars. Following from the design of the Thinline electrics, Ted McCarty came up with the idea of incorporating a solid maple block inside a guitar's body to blend the resonance of a hollow-body with the sustain of a solidbody. A slimmed-down body depth

GIBSON's peak output of the original gold-top (this example, right, has new tuners) occurred in 1953 when a little over 2200 units were made, beaten only by the LG-1 flat-top and the electric ES-125. Gibson's highest-yet production figure would come in 1959 when 4364 Les Paul Juniors were shipped.

THE SWITCH above the neck selects between pickups. The upper position (marked 'Rhythm') gives front pickup; the lower position ('Treble') selects the rear pickup; and the central position, as shown here, provides both pickups.

1st Annual Combo Issue

DOWN BEAT ®

July 15, 1953

Richard
Rodgers
Sounds Off
(See Page 3)

★ ★ ★

Sauter,
Finegan,
& Goldfish
(See Page 2)

★ ★ ★

'Star Night'
Cast
Complete
(See Page 1)

★ ★ ★

On The Cover

Les Paul,
Mary Ford

DURING the first half of the 1950s Les Paul was the most famous guitarist in America. Despite moving from his jazz roots to achieve a string of pop hits with singer Mary Ford, Paul could still make the cover of the top jazz magazine Down Beat (left). Paul invariably modified the guitars that Gibson sent him: note the unusual knobs and the crude vibrato of this gold-top.

and a graceful double-cutaway shape that gave unparalleled access to the 22-fret neck contributed to the superior functionality of the new model. Along with the stereo ES-345T and the ES-355T, a new genre of electrics was born: the semi-acoustic (or semi-solid) guitar.

The 1950s saw the coming of age of the electric guitar. In a matter of years, electrics looked and sounded like nothing else before, while similarly dramatic changes affected the music. This formative period witnessed the transition from 'electrified' to electric guitar, and by the end of the 1950s solidbody and Thinline electrics had surpassed full-body archtops in popularity. In this highly challenging and competitive context, Gibson introduced many historically significant designs which are still firm favorites today. ■ ANDRE DUCHOSSOIR

CLOCK RADIOS are introduced, waking folks with such news as Republican 'Ike' Eisenhower's inauguration as 34th US president, the end of the Korean war, the conquest of Mount Everest, and Queen Elizabeth II's coronation.

CRAZY MAN CRAZY by Bill Haley & his Comets is arguably the first hit rock'n'roll record, reaching number 12 in May.

LUNG CANCER is reported as attributable to cigarette smoking; meanwhile L&M still advertise their cigarettes as "just what the doctor ordered".

COLOR TV is demonstrated for the first time when NBC broadcast a test transmission using three trial systems beamed from the Empire State Building in New York.

JUKEBOX favorites include Willie Mae Thornton's 'Hound Dog', an early take on country rock with a rip-roaring guitar solo by Pete Lewis of Johnny Otis' band. The Leiber & Stoller song will later provide a big hit for Elvis Presley.

JAMES BOND debuts in Ian Fleming's first novel, Casino Royale... but not in Simone De Beauvoir's seminal feminist work, The Second Sex.

△ GIBSON LES PAUL 'GOLD-TOP'
Produced 1952-58, 1968-72, re-issued 1985; this example 1957.

More changes were made to the gold-top during the later 1950s: in 1955 Gibson's new adjustable Tune-o-matic bridge was fitted, improving intonation, while two years later the company's new noise-canceling humbucking pickups were added. Left-handed guitars were made to special order and in small numbers; this rare left-handed gold-top is owned today by Paul McCartney.

△ GIBSON LES PAUL 'GOLD-TOP'
Produced 1952-58, 1968-72, re-issued 1985; this example 1954.

The 'trapeze' tailpiece fitted to the original gold-top (see page 17) was quickly replaced with this bar-type in 1953, when Gibson also increased the angle at which the neck met the body. These changes overcame criticisms of the original's limited sustain and inaccurate intonation, and made hand-damping effects possible.

DECALS were silk-screened on to the holly wood veneer of the headstock face (above). While 'Les Paul Model' was the name used by Gibson for the gold Les Paul, aficionados refer to the guitar as the 'gold-top'.

DEAD: Django Reinhardt, Dylan Thomas, Joseph Stalin. Born: Tom Petty, Mike Oldfield, Robert Cray.

JAZZ GUITARS *by Charles Alexander*

When Charlie Christian joined the Benny Goodman band in 1939 the electric guitar was almost unknown in jazz, and yet just over a decade later, as the 1950s dawned, jazz guitarists were rarely to be heard without the assistance of an amplifier. Jazz guitar music revealed its public faces and its musicians' musicians, from Barney Kessel to Johnny Smith, as players wrestled with old-school swing, still hip bop and the latest strains of cool and modern jazz.

Barney Kessel

Tenderly
Just Squeeze Me
Bernardo
Vicky's Dream
Salute to Charlie Christian
What is There to Say
Lullaby of Birdland
I Let a Song Go Out of My Heart

vogue
RECORDS
L.D.E. 085

THE BEST-KNOWN jazz guitarist of the 1950s was Barney Kessel (above). Kessel's first influence was the early electric jazz guitarist Charlie Christian, and in a 1953 interview Kessel repeated Christian's advice to him: "If you can make some interesting harmony after you know how to swing, that's fine. But to begin with, swing alone is enough to

JAZZ GUITAR

Charlie Christian's swinging, horn-like lines and the sound of his hollow-body Gibson with its bar pickup had inspired a generation of guitarists to amplify. By 1950, eight years after Christian's premature death at the age of 25, the electric guitar was commonplace in jazz.

Prior to Charlie Christian the jazz guitar had been primarily a rhythm section instrument and guitar players were rarely permitted to play solos. Now the guitar, like the piano, could function both in the rhythm section and the front line. At the same time there was an economic motive for guitarists to amplify and to sharpen their soloing skills, as the decline of the large swing orchestras was putting the traditional acoustic rhythm guitarist out of work.

The emergence of the electric guitar as a jazz instrument in the 1940s had coincided with the bebop revolution, spearheaded by saxophonist Charlie Parker and trumpeter Dizzy Gillespie. This new form of jazz, with its fast tempos and rhythmic and harmonic complexity, demanded far greater technical skills than the earlier swing style. Charlie Christian's jazz lines and phrasing were rooted in swing, rather than bebop, and bear the influence of the great swing-era saxophonist Lester Young. Most of the major jazz guitarists of the 1950s acknowledged Charlie

GIBSON's hollow-body electrics generally came finished either in sunburst (as here) or natural.

THE ES-175D was at first fitted with a pair of Gibson's P90 pickups (as on the example above), but during 1957 the company's new noise-canceling humbucking pickups began to appear on Gibson guitars, including the 175D.

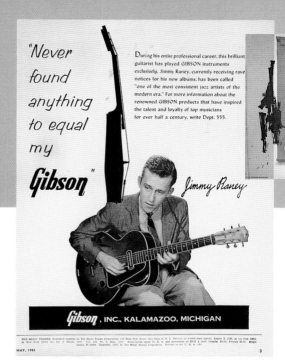

"Never found anything to equal my Gibson"

Jimmy Raney

During his entire professional career, this brilliant guitarist has played GIBSON instruments exclusively. Jimmy Raney, currently receiving rave notices for his new albums, has been called "one of the most consistent jazz artists of the modern era." For more information about the renowned GIBSON products that have inspired the talent and loyalty of top musicians for over half a century, write Dept. 555.

Gibson, INC., KALAMAZOO, MICHIGAN

JIM HALL's wonderfully understated playing on a Gibson ES-175D was at large in the 1950s on his own solo albums (center left). Herb Ellis (left) was also a Gibson ES-175 man, opting for a single-pickup version.

JIMMY RANEY, master of the 1950s 'cool' school of jazz playing, is often seen (as above and inset) with a Gibson ES-150 guitar, the company's original electric-acoustic hollow-body design that dates back to the mid-1930s.

Christian as their primary inspiration, and elements of this pioneer's style are in evidence in the hard-swinging, bluesy styles of Barney Kessel and Herb Ellis.

Barney Kessel was born in 1923. He grew up in Muskogee, Oklahoma, and from an early age was fascinated by the blues and jazz he heard around him. He bought his first guitar at age 12 and within two years was playing with a local jazz group – the only white musician in the band. Many touring bands passed through the area

and Kessel would jam with the musicians after hours. Hearing word of this remarkable young guitarist, Charlie Christian came to Muskogee to hear the 16-year-old Kessel play. This visit from his idol encouraged Kessel in his chosen career and within a year he had left for Los Angeles.

By the time he recorded his first album as a leader in 1953 when he was 30, Kessel was already a seasoned performer. He'd worked with the big bands of Chico Marx, Artie Shaw, Charlie Barnet and Benny Goodman, recorded with Charlie Parker and Billie Holiday and toured the US and Europe with the Oscar Peterson Trio. A mainstay of LA's busy radio and television recording scene, Kessel was also in demand as an accompanist for leading jazz vocalists such as Sarah Vaughan, Ella Fitzgerald and Anita O'Day. His guitar introduction and backup on Julie London's 1955 recording of 'Cry Me A River' is legendary.

In short, Barney was the best-known and most popular jazz guitarist in the US during the 1950s, topping the jazz guitar polls year after year in magazines such as Down Beat and Esquire. This led to a series of superb Poll Winners albums for the Contemporary label with bassist Ray Brown and drummer Shelly Manne, which established the guitar trio format and also demonstrated the range of expression of which the electric guitar is capable in jazz: from delicate

chord melody ballads to driving, blues-laced single-line solos. From the late 1960s until the early 1990s, when he suffered a stroke and could no longer play, Kessel pursued an active touring career with his trio and, from 1974 together with Herb Ellis and Charlie Byrd, as a member of the Great Guitars.

Herb Ellis was born in Texas in 1921, and his career began to follow a similar pattern to Kessel's – indeed their paths have at times intertwined. Ellis's big break came when he followed Kessel into the Oscar Peterson Trio in 1953. Ellis fitted in perfectly and stayed for five years. One of the best four-in-the-bar rhythm guitarists anywhere, Ellis drew pulsing chordal work from his Gibson ES-175, compensating for the lack of drums. He could negotiate Peterson's complex arrangements and solos quite convincingly, while never losing his earthy, bluesy quality at even the fastest of tempos.

The Trio toured incessantly and recorded extensively with many of the top jazz artists of the time, giving Ellis a high profile which opened the door to a two-year stint with vocalist Ella Fitzgerald and 17 years in the Los Angeles studios, where he would play on movie scores and on weekly television shows, while also performing on countless record dates.

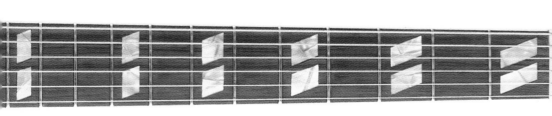

THESE ANGLED fingerboard markers are usually referred to as 'split parallelogram' types.

THE SO-CALLED 'crown' headstock inlay (above) was used by Gibson on nearly every one of the ES line of electric-acoustic instruments.

△ GIBSON ES-175D

Produced 1953-current; this example 1953

Gibson first issued the hollow-body ES-175 as a single-pickup guitar in 1949, but within four years introduced the optional ES-175D model which was fitted with two pickups and the necessary extra controls (the 'D' in the model name stands for double pickups). The 175 has become prominent over the decades primarily as a jazz guitar, and it has long been Gibson's best-selling electric-acoustic guitar. The sharp cutaway of the model was unique on a Gibson instrument for some years, and the ES-175 popularized a pressed, laminated maple/basswood body which contributes to its distinctively bright sound.

In the *Gibson* galaxy of stars!

KENNY BURRELL talented young guitarist, now leading his own quartet, is plucking his way to fame on his Gibson. Fascinating LP's on Blue Note and Prestige labels plus night spot and air wave dates, with such greats as Benny Goodman, Oscar Peterson and Hampton Hawes, landed Kenny among the big popularity poll winners.

Gibson INC.
KALAMAZOO, MICHIGAN

MASON'S MUSIC
1555 EGLINTON AVE. W. & 580 BAYVIEW AVE.

KENNY BURRELL (with ES-175, left) grew up in Detroit in a musical family and, taking up the guitar at age 12, was inspired by jazz guitarists Charlie Christian and Oscar Moore, but also by bluesmen such as Lightning Hopkins, Muddy Waters and T-Bone Walker. These influences are reflected in Burrell's sophisticated blend of hard-swinging bebop lines, soulful bluesy statements and rich

chordal passages. After a six-month stint with Oscar Peterson, he settled in New York in 1956 and made his first solo album the following year. Soon he was one of the busiest jazz guitarists on the New York scene, recording with a wide range of artists including Duke Ellington and John Coltrane, and making several classic albums as a leader, such as Midnight Blue, and Guitar Forms.

JOHNNY SMITH (right) rose to fame through a 1952 recording with Stan Getz of 'Moonlight In Vermont', complete with Smith's clear, reverb-tinged sound, his fleet-fingered but relaxed three-octave runs, and above all his lush, close-voiced, chord melody style. In 1956 Guild produced the Johnny Smith Award archtop acoustic (with add-on pickup, right). This was based on the guitarist's favored D'Angelico guitar, but Smith disliked the result and did not take up the Guild. Gibson produced a Johnny Smith model in 1961. Smith retired from performing in the mid 1970s to concentrate on his music store business.

Guild
JOHNNY SMITH AWARD MODEL Guitar
(In Limited Production Only)

ROOST LP 2216
Hi-Fidelity

THE NEW Johnny Smith QUARTET

GUILD's Stuart model, like many archtop Guilds, came in two finishes which were distinguished by different model numbers. The Stuart, for example, was known as the X-500 in sunburst, while the natural version (like this example) was the X-550.

THE HARP-STYLE tailpiece (above) was a distinctive feature of many Guild guitars, made for the US company by Müller in Germany.

GRETSCH (below) used plain, pearl and sparkle plastic finishes on drums, so why not on guitars as well?

△ GUILD STUART X-550
Produced 1953-current; this example 1958

Guild was started in New York in 1952 by Alfred Dronge and George Mann along with a team of mainly ex-Epiphone workers who had decided not to move to Philadelphia with their old company. Guild, who in 1956 also moved out of New York City (to Hoboken, New Jersey), was best known through the 1950s for high quality archtop guitars, of which the Stuart X-550 electric model was top of the line, while in the 1960s Guild's flat-top acoustics were also well regarded. The company changed hands several times, and in 1995 was bought by Fender.

THE KAY Musical Instrument Company was established in Chicago in the early 1930s, growing from Stromberg-Voisinet which was run by Henry Kay Kuhrmeyer and whose most popular guitar line was called Kay-Kraft. By 1935 the Kay company was based in Walnut Street, Chicago.

△ KAY THIN TWIN K161
Produced 1953-1958; t his example 1954

The K161's more friendly name came from its 'Thin' body and 'Twin' pickups, and Kay was proud of what it called the "new type body construction": hollow maple, but with a central block of wood running from neck to tailpiece on which to mount the two single-coil pickups.

V-SHAPED markers (below) recall Guild craftsmen's earlier work with Epiphone.

AS NEW
as new can be!

Here's an entirely new kind of Spanish electric guitar, the Kay "Twin Thin." Two high fidelity pick-ups, each with separate tone and volume controls, permit you to accentuate bass, treble or both. Just flip the 3-way selector switch for the effect you want! New type body construction for sustained tones. Lightweight. For free folder, write Kay, 1640 Walnut St., Chicago 12, Illinois.

KAY
THIN TWIN
"ELECTRIC"

3-WAY SELECTOR SWITCH
TWIN TONE CONTROLS
TWIN VOLUME CONTROLS

KAY's 1930s founder Henry Kay Kuhrmeyer sold his company in 1955 to a group of investors including former Harmony manager Sidney M. Katz, and by the end of the 1950s Kay had become one of the largest guitar producers in the US. Most Kay instruments were aimed at beginners and were of average quality, designed to sell at competitive prices. The Thin Twin (a 1953 ad is shown, left) was a good example of how Kay would echo existing market trends – it was a thin, lightweight, solidbody-style instrument – with lower-priced alternatives.

Later in the 1950s Jim Hall, a graduate of the Cleveland Institute of Music, attracted much attention when in 1958 he joined the innovative Chico Hamilton Quintet. Since that time Hall has been one of the most distinctive voices in jazz guitar. At the end of the 1950s saxophonist Jimmy Giuffre invited Hall to join his drum-less trio. This group, renowned for its 'Train And The River' theme, was featured in the movie Jazz On A Summer's Day, filmed at the 1959 Newport Jazz Festival.

A masterful improviser with an unerring sense of melodic development, Hall possesses an instinct for understatement that distinguishes him from the majority of guitar players. With Hall every note counts, and space and color play an important role. His sound is clear and mellow (on earlier recordings from a Gibson ES-175 but more

recently from a D'Aquisto), but he doesn't shy away from dissonance or earthy, bluesy phrases. These qualities, together with Hall's sympathetic and harmonically informed accompaniments, have led him into fruitful musical partnerships with vocalist Ella Fitzgerald, with saxophonists Sonny Rollins and Paul Desmond, with trumpeters Chet Baker and Art Farmer and with bassists Red Mitchell and Ron Carter, and his early 1960s duo recordings with pianist Bill Evans are widely regarded as high points in the careers of both these musicians.

The Hollywood studios offered many 1950s musicians an attractive financial alternative to the precarious living to be made on the jazz scene. Howard Roberts (1929-1992) was already a fluent, driving jazz guitarist when he moved to Los Angeles from Phoenix, Arizona, but was soon

making a living "as an industrial guitarist", to use his own phrase, and his versatile guitar work crops up in countless TV and movie soundtracks from The Flintstones to The Sandpiper and on albums accompanying artists from Elvis Presley to Peggy Lee. By night Howard was performing on the LA jazz scene with leading artists such as Dexter Gordon, Bud Shank, Al Haig and Chico Hamilton, and in 1955 he won Down Beat magazine's New Star award.

Curious about every type of music from traditional blues to contemporary rock and classical music, Roberts made a thorough and valuable study of harmony, counterpoint and composition. A series of albums on Verve and Capitol underlines his versatility and his willingness to experiment with orchestral settings and rock contexts. Roberts wrote several practical handbooks for guitarists including Howard

△ GRETSCH SILVER JET
Produced 1954-1963, re-issued 1989; this example 1955

In 1953 Gretsch launched its first 'solidbody' electric, the Duo-Jet – actually a semi-solid concoction with a pressed top – and the following year applied a sparkle plastic finish courtesy of its drum department for a chintzy partner, the Silver Jet.

THE GRETSCH logo with a large T (above) used during the 1950s and after is described by collectors as the 'T roof' logo.

COLORFUL finishes became a distinctive element of Gretsch's guitars in the 1950s with models such as the green Country Club and the sparkling Silver Jet (far left). Gretsch exploited this in publicity; a catalog from 1955 (left) shows a trio of bright semi-solid models, the red Jet Fire Bird, black Duo-Jet and orange Round Up.

RCA Hits Disc Bootleggers

DOWN BEAT

August

the Swinging Guitar of TAL FARLOW

End Of 78 RPMs Nearing? (See Page 1)

Big Year For Pianists (See Page 2)

On The Cover Red Norvo Trio

25 cents
CANADA 20c
FOREIGN 35c

TAL FARLOW's lightning bebop lines caused a stir in the 1950s, not least in the Red Norvo Trio; seen (far left) on the cover of Down Beat, Farlow is in front of bassist Charlie Mingus and alongside Norvo, the group's vibraphone-playing leader. Farlow also had a fine solo career, his LPs including Swinging Guitar (1956, left), the cover of which featured his Gibson ES-350.

Roberts Chord Melody, Howard Roberts Guitar Book, Howard Roberts Super Chops and the 3-volume Praxis Guitar Compendium. In later years, Roberts co-founded with Pat Hicks the Guitar Institute of Technology in Los Angeles and wrote its original syllabus.

For players such as Tal Farlow and Jimmy Raney, it was the bebop lines of saxophonist Charlie Parker and pianists Bud Powell and Al Haig that figured most prominently in their musical development. Farlow, who grew up in Greensboro, North Carolina, relied on the radio to hear the popular music of the day and became fascinated by the virtuoso jazz pianist Art Tatum. Farlow particularly admired the way that Tatum would vary the harmonies of a song, and began to explore similar ideas on the guitar. Moving to New York in 1944 he witnessed the bebop revolution at first hand and absorbed the playing of Charlie Parker, Dizzy Gillespie, Bud Powell and Miles Davis into his own work.

By the time Farlow joined the Red Norvo Trio in 1949 he was already a fine player but, rising to the musical challenge presented by vibraphonist Norvo, Farlow worked hard on his technique and developed the ability to play long, flowing bebop lines at ultra-fast tempos. He also became a master at playing complete solos using artificial harmonics. Farlow's four years with Norvo introduced him to a wide audience and confirmed his standing as an innovative jazz guitarist. A succession of excellent albums throughout the 1950s showed a player of exceptional technique and creative powers who could re-harmonize a song with the most sophisticated chord melody arrangement and then follow it with chorus after chorus of inventive, swinging improvisation.

In 1950 Farlow developed a short-scale guitar by reducing the length of the neck in order to enable bigger left-hand stretches. This allowed more unusual chord voicings, but also reduced string tension. A decade later he would collaborate with Gibson on the design of their Tal Farlow model, with its distinctive scrolled cutaway.

Unlike many of his contemporaries, Tal was never attracted by the lure of commercial studio work and, in spite of a period away from the spotlight during the 1960s, he has made his musical career solely in jazz. Still active in the mid-1990s, he remains possibly the most influential of those jazz guitarists whose careers flowered in the 1950s. Many later players, among them John McLaughlin and Pat Martino, have quoted Tal Farlow as a primary inspiration.

While Tal Farlow was applying the hard-bop idiom to the guitar in the late 1940s and the 1950s, Jimmy Raney was

SIMPLICITY ruled in the design of the Les Paul Junior (below) as Gibson competed with lower-priced guitars.

GIBSON's Les Paul Junior had a solid mahogany body and a rosewood fingerboard.

A CUSTOMER in 1956 could buy all six Gibson electrics in this Kansas City shop window (right), including the Les Paul Junior, for $1610. Today they'd fetch around $20,000.

GUILD never attracted the same caliber of players to endorse its guitars in the 1950s as did Gibson, despite a brief but unsuccessful collaboration with Johnny Smith (see p22). It's hard to imagine that ads like the 1959 example for the X-350 shown (left) did much to widen the appeal of Guild's guitars.

△ GUILD STRATFORD X-350
Produced 1954-1965; this example 1954

This Guild model emphasized the earlier connections of the company's workers with Epiphone, being very similar in pickup and control layout to the Zephyr Emperor Regent model (see p8).

RIGHT-WING Republican senator Joseph McCarthy is discredited by the US Senate. A wave of anti-Communist hysteria, blacklists and McCarthy's investigations committee were unleashed after his unsubstantiated claim in 1950 that the State Department was infiltrated by Communists.

GIBSON guitars were by far the most prominent among the instruments used by the leading jazz guitar players of the 1950s. Of the guitarists in the prestigious Down Beat poll for 1956, for example, Gibson could count six of the top ten as being 'their' players: Barney Kessel, Tal Farlow, Les Paul, Herb Ellis (above), Jimmy Raney and Jim Hall.

approaching it from a different angle. From Louisville, Kentucky, Raney began his professional career in New York in 1944 at the age of 17 when he joined the Jerry Wald Orchestra. The bebop movement was transforming jazz music then, adding fresh harmonic and rhythmic ideas and introducing a rich repertoire of compositions. Studying at first hand the playing of its leading exponents, among them saxophonist Charlie Parker and pianists Bud Powell and Al Haig, Raney worked out a way to apply their complex lines to the guitar.

Raney's gently swinging style combined clarity with harmonic subtlety. Long, flowing, improvised lines, sparkling with surprises, would weave their way through the outer reaches of the harmonies – always melodic but never obvious. Raney's reputation as an innovative guitar

stylist was established through the recordings he made with saxophonist Stan Getz in 1952 and was confirmed by his subsequent albums with Red Norvo, Bob Brookmeyer, Zoot Sims, Jim Hall and others. Particularly outstanding are the 12 tracks he recorded in Paris in 1954 with a French rhythm section while on tour there with the Red Norvo Trio.

In the 1970s, after several years off the jazz scene back in his home town of Louisville, Jimmy teamed up with his son Doug, also a fine guitarist. Touring worldwide, he opened up a fresh and creative phase in his career. Increasing deafness and deteriorating health forced him to stop touring in the late 1980s, however, and Jimmy Raney, the master of the 'cool school' of jazz guitar, died in May 1995. ■ CHARLES ALEXANDER

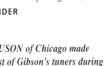

DESPITE containing just six per cent of the world's population, the US has 34% of its railways, 58% of the telephones and 60% of the cars.

▽ GIBSON LES PAUL JUNIOR
Produced 1954-1961; this example 1956

Once Gibson established that its $225 Les Paul gold-top model would sell, it came out with a cheaper solidbody, the plain, slab-body, single-pickup, sunburst Junior, at just $99.50.

KLUSON of Chicago made most of Gibson's tuners during the 1950s, including these cheap three-on-a-plate types.

TRANSISTOR RADIOS are introduced, made by Regency.

DOO-WOP heaven as The Spaniels make 'Goodnight Sweetheart Goodnight' and The Penguins record 'Earth Angel'. Meanwhile, Elvis Presley makes his first recordings.

IN THE UK, food rationing officially ends, celebrated by a bonfire of ration books in London. In the US, the term 'fast food' comes into use.

CUSTOMS of the first few years feature a P90 pickup at the bridge and a more powerful Alnico type at the neck (below).

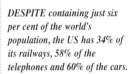

△ GIBSON LES PAUL CUSTOM
Produced 1954-1961, 1968-current; this example 1956

As well as the lower-priced Junior, Gibson expanded its Les Paul line upwards in 1954 with the classy $325 all-black Custom, complete with multiple binding and gold-plated hardware.

WEST GERMANY win the soccer World Cup, beating favorites Hungary 5-1. Roger Gilbert Bannister, a 25-year-old British medical student, runs the first sub-four-minute mile.

THE FENDER STORY *by Walter Carter*

Pop music of the 1950s bolted away from the smooth and cerebral Sinatra, the refined crooner, and toward the raucous and raw Elvis, with his most basic, unrefined expressions of emotion. So too guitar makers began the decade pushing the electric archtop tradition to its highest level of refinement, only to be undermined and toppled by a plain, uncrafted creation that reduced the electric guitar to its most basic form. That creation was the Fender guitar.

THE FENDER STORY

The silhouette of a Fender Stratocaster would become by the end of the decade an icon for rock'n'roll music, but at the beginning of 1950 the Fender Electric Instrument Co. was a little company in Fullerton, California, that didn't even make a standard electric guitar. Just as no one could have predicted rock'n'roll, no one — not even Leo Fender himself — could have predicted the coming revolution that Fender's solidbody electric guitars would lead.

Clarence Leo Fender was a most unlikely revolutionary: a low-key, somewhat reclusive man; an accountant by training, a radio repairman by vocation. He never even learned to tune a guitar, much less play one. He and his early partner Doc Kauffman had made a crude, virtually unplayable solidbody electric in 1943 to test a pickup design, but the products of the business he started immediately after World War II were small guitar amps and the simplest sort of electric guitar, the Hawaiian 'lap steel'. Leo's business started so small that, according to Fender lore, he baked the finishes on early instruments in Kauffman's kitchen oven. Fender steels were plain — the antithesis of the flashy Gibsons and Nationals of the time.

In the late 1940s Leo decided to apply these simple, proletarian designs to a standard or 'Spanish-neck' electric guitar. Given the look of his Hawaiians, it's likely that his decision to make his guitar with a solid rather than hollow body was based as much on practical considerations — he was not in a financial position to tool up and produce conventional hollow-body archtop instruments, nor to challenge the major manufacturers on their own turf — as it was on some grand vision of the solidbody electric guitar as the vehicle of the future for popular music.

Fender's solidbody electric guitar, dubbed the Esquire, was introduced at a 1950 trade show. Like Leo's early lap steels, it had a homemade aura, with a single pickup (Gibson's latest had three), a flat-topped 'slab' body that any woodshop student could cut out on a bandsaw, a maple neck that didn't even have a separate fingerboard or a truss rod, and a sickly maple-colored paint job that let the grain of the ash wood show through (although one or more of the originals may have been black-painted pine). The guitar industry laughed at Fender's 'plank' or 'toilet-seat' guitar and continued to put pickups on hollow-body archtop guitars.

Sales of the Esquire and the subsequent two-pickup model, the Telecaster (née Broadcaster), were slow: about 1000 to 1500 a year, according to Don Randall, Leo's partner in Fender Sales, which had been formed to market Fender instruments. "The backbone of the business was the lap-top steel guitars, the double-necks and the triple-necks," Randall says. "After the Stratocaster came out and after the Precision Bass came out, of course rock'n'roll was beginning and kids were teaching each other to play instead of going to [teaching] studios, and then the thing became more or less geometric in its take-off."

Bill Carson, a country artist who was playing guitar in the early 1950s for Hank Thompson, was an early evangelist for Fender. "I started hanging out there and being somewhat partially reimbursed for expenses by Leo

FENDER's advertising during the 1950s was far superior to that of the average guitar manufacturer, not only in press ads (like the cool cat of 1957, below) but also in the company's catalogs and general promotional material.

△ FENDER STRATOCASTER
Produced 1954-current; this example 1956

Fender's Stratocaster first appeared in 1954, when its sleek lines and contoured body proved a shocking and futuristic departure from conventional guitar design. A vibrato-equipped version like this sold then for $249.50, or $20 less without vibrato ('hardtail' as it's now nicknamed). The Strat's distinctive looks, crisp sounds and easy playability would soon make it a world-beater.

DON RANDALL *ran the all-important Fender Sales operation, which had been formed in 1953 when Fender's existing sales arrangement with Radio & Television Equipment*

Co. was re-organized. Randall is seen (below) in a new Piper Apache aircraft purchased by Fender Sales in 1957 and which Randall would pilot on cross-country sales trips.

KEY PERSONNEL *(left) at the Fender company during the 1950s included George Fullerton (left) who had started in 1948, Freddie Tavares (center) who came on board in 1953 and was strongly involved in the development of new instruments such as the Strat and later Jazzmaster, and Forrest White (right) who joined a year later to run the Fender factory.*

to do prototypes, take them out and play them myself and also leave them in clubs now and then," he said. Jimmy Bryant, the hot-picking country guitarist who recorded legendary duets with steel guitarist Speedy West, was an early convert, and Fender gained a foothold in country music that would in time lead to domination.

The Telecaster was not without problems, some of which related to the guitar's simple three-section bridge. As

Carson said in 1995, "You couldn't tune it then; you can't tune it now." Carson also disliked the sharp edge of the Telecaster's unembellished slab body, which dug into his ribs. He and another southern California country guitarist, Rex Gallion, are credited with suggesting contours in the back and top so that the guitar would, in Carson's words, "fit you like a shirt". "They didn't really want to build the guitar that I wanted them to build, which ended up being

THE STRAT's *headstock (below right) was probably influenced by the design of an earlier Paul Bigsby guitar, which in turn seems to be based on European headstocks of the early 19th century.*

△ FENDER STRATOCASTER
Produced 1954-current; this example 1954

This famous guitar, owned by David Gilmour of Pink Floyd, bears serial number 0001 – but it is not the first Stratocaster made. Fender components are often dated, and this Strat's neck is dated May 1954, the vibrato cavity June, a month or two after production began. More likely this was a special-order guitar – it has a non-standard colored finish and gold-plated hardware – that was made even more special with a one-off serial number.

EARLY STRATS *can come with gold-colored anodized aluminum pickguards (like the example above). While these provided good electrical shielding, their electrolytic anodized 'skin' tended to wear through, leaving unsightly patches, and they were quickly replaced with plastic units.*

SYNCHRONIZED

Tremolo Action...

in the new "Comfort Contoured"
Stratocaster

ANOTHER "FIRST" FOR *Fender!*

First again in the field of amplified music . . . thrilling new "Stratocaster" by Fender! Unequalled in design — unequalled in performance . . . a flick of the wrist means live, vibrant — perfect pitch.

There's a thrill in store for you when you see this revolutionary new instrument. Three pick-ups, a special tone control, a new surface mounted plug . . . all mean faster action, better, clearer music . . . whether you play it "straight" or while using the revolutionary Tremolo Action lever.

The Stratocaster features advanced design in body too! Here is an instrument actually "comfort contoured" for you! Its engineered to fit the artists body . . . designed to be "part of the player."

See the new, revolutionary Fender Stratocaster at your dealer soon . . . play it . . . and be the first to experience this new amplified music thrill!

The "Stratocaster" is available with or without "Tremolo" Action.

Write for our latest brochure and name of nearest dealer.

PROMOTION *for Fender's new Stratocaster guitar began to appear in the first half of 1954, such as this trade press ad (right) from May. Here the accent is on the new guitar's "revolutionary Tremolo*

Action lever", in fact the world's first self-contained vibrato unit: an integrated adjustable bridge, tailpiece and vibrato system which provided the Strat player with pitchbend and shimmering chord effects.

Fender
SALES, INC.   308 EAST FIFTH STREET   SANTA ANA, CALIFORNIA

The "CHIRPING" CRICKETS

BUDDY HOLLY (second from right) fronted the first truly self-contained pop group, The Crickets, who wrote most of their own material, played virtually all the instruments on their records, and performed live as a group. Holly's gleaming Stratocaster was almost as notable a visual trademark as his horn-rimmed specs, and the guitar's

appearance on an early sleeve design (left) had many a fledgling guitarist poring over its unfamiliar outline, the Strat seeming especially futuristic when compared to the staid and old-fashioned look of the Gibson hollow-body electric pictured alongside. Holly more than any other player in the 1950s established the Strat as a sleek, desirable, modern guitar.

▽ FENDER STRATOCASTER
Produced 1954-current; this example 1959

Having started the decade without a Spanish electric, Fender had eight models by the time this guitar was made in 1959: the Esquire, Telecaster, Strat, Duo-Sonic, Musicmaster, Jazzmaster, and bound-body Custom Esquire and Custom Telecaster.

STRATS in colors other than the standard sunburst were sold on a limited, ad-hoc basis until 1956, when Fender first listed 'player's choice' colors as an option. In the following year these Du Pont paint finishes, as used on many General Motors cars, were called 'custom colors' by Fender, a name that has stuck ever since.

THIS 'FIESTA RED' (above) was one of Fender's earliest custom colors. Original colored Strats from the 1950s are rare.

the Stratocaster, because they didn't want to tool up for it," Carson says. "The company was pretty poor at that time."

In sales, Don Randall was also pushing for a new guitar to compete with the gold-top Les Paul that Gibson had introduced in 1952. "The Telecaster was a plain slab guitar," he explains. "We had to have a prettier guitar. The Stratocaster evolved from that."

Fender's new guitar of 1954 fulfilled all requests. A six-piece saddle allowed individual string adjustment. A 'tremolo' (vibrato) system returned the strings to true pitch. The body shape was a fluid, modernistic double-cutaway with contoured back and top. There were three pickups, probably not due to any players' demands for more tonal

possibilities, but simply because the Fender team felt that three pickups surely had to be better than two.

Randall was the staff model-namer: "I named the Broadkaster, because at that time radio was the big thing," he says. "We were just coming into the television field. When Fred Gretsch called me and said they owned the name Broadkaster [used on Gretsch drums], then television was the next thing – Telecaster. Stratocaster – the next highest thing would be the stratosphere."

Carson, the guinea pig for Leo's experiments, recalls the prototype Stratocaster. "The bridge was backwards, where you had to stick a screwdriver under the string to adjust it. I broke one [string] the first night I had it in a club. The

screws adjusted from the neck side, and it's almost impossible to get a screwdriver under there. I had an easier time when we got that bridgeplate reversed.

"The guitar was very crude," he adds, "with no finish on it, no plated parts on it, but it played in tune all the way down the neck, and every session player in that part of the country, of which there were not very many at the time, would borrow that guitar. I had a hard time getting it back from them."

Unlike the slow-starting Telecaster, the Strat came blazing out of the blocks. "Solidbody guitars were beginning to move pretty well at that time," Randall says, "and when we came out with this one it was quite an innovation, with the

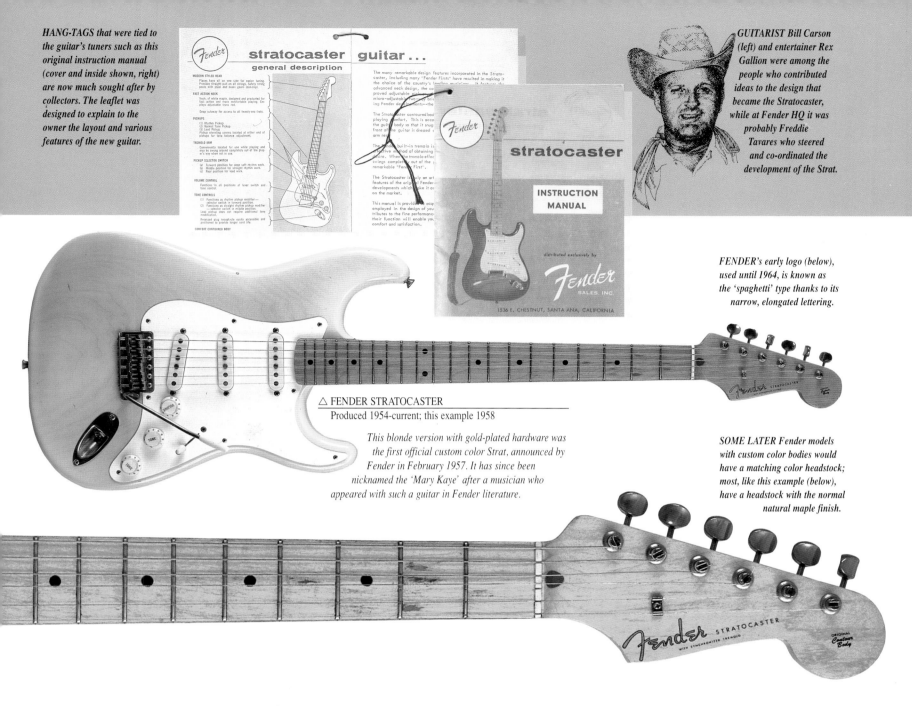

HANG-TAGS that were tied to the guitar's tuners such as this original instruction manual (cover and inside shown, right) are now much sought after by collectors. The leaflet was designed to explain to the owner the layout and various features of the new guitar.

GUITARIST Bill Carson (left) and entertainer Rex Gallion were among the people who contributed ideas to the design that became the Stratocaster, while at Fender HQ it was probably Freddie Tavares who steered and co-ordinated the development of the Strat.

△ FENDER STRATOCASTER
Produced 1954-current; this example 1958

This blonde version with gold-plated hardware was the first official custom color Strat, announced by Fender in February 1957. It has since been nicknamed the 'Mary Kaye' after a musician who appeared with such a guitar in Fender literature.

FENDER's early logo (below), used until 1964, is known as the 'spaghetti' type thanks to its narrow, elongated lettering.

SOME LATER Fender models with custom color bodies would have a matching color headstock; most, like this example (below), have a headstock with the normal natural maple finish.

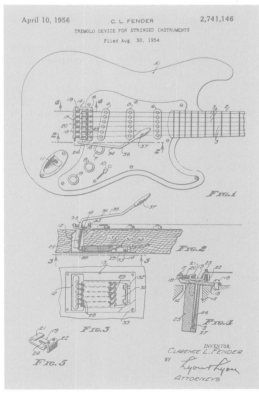

THIS PATENT (left), filed in summer 1954, concerns the Stratocaster's vibrato system, or 'tremolo device for stringed instruments' as it's described. The Fender team had been through much anguish to get the system (described by one insider as "Leo's pride and joy") to a manufacturable state, and at one stage they had to junk several thousand dollars'

worth of tooling. Leo Fender, under his full name of Clarence L Fender, registered a number of other patents during the 1950s relating to various guitar parts and designs, including the bridge and pickup assembly of the Telecaster (patent filed in January 1950; see p14), and the Jazzmaster's offset-waist body (filed in January 1958).

cutaway in the back and the lopped-off front so you didn't have to move your arm. It had a lot of features you could talk about, and it did have the sound. We didn't have any trouble selling them. We sold them by the jillions."

The Stratocaster was the most refined guitar of its day, a masterful combination of aesthetics and functionality, and although it would be followed by more 'refinements' such as the Jazzmaster model, it would eventually emerge as an even greater achievement than its creators ever imagined. "I've watched this over the years," Carson says, "and a country player, a Western swing player, wouldn't be caught dead playing what a rock'n'roll player played, and vice versa. Finally the Strat just transgressed

all these things. It put to bed once and for all the fact that there is one guitar that will do it."

The Telecaster and Stratocaster are enough to qualify Fender as the leading light of the 1950s, but these models had a solid supporting cast — Fender amplifiers and the Fender Precision Bass — that allowed the guitars and the guitarists to break easily through conventional barriers, particularly in the area of volume. Fender guitars were louder than conventional hollow-body electrics... but 'loud guitar' is a bit of a simplification. The solid bodies gave Fenders an inherent capability for more sound with less feedback, but beyond that, 'loud guitar' really means 'loud amplifier'. Fender's amps — which were Leo's own real specialty — were the industry standard, regardless of what kind of guitar you played (Buddy Holly being the notable, ironic exception, playing his Strat through a Magnatone amp).

Amps, Don Randall says, "were the mainstay of the whole music business. It was through Fender amplifiers that all these bands became amplified. With the advent of the solidbody guitar and the amplifier it was the first time the guitar player could drown out the drummer. The amplifiers were the big factor. However, as it developed, the sales of guitars and amplifiers dollar-wise about paralleled each other after the initial period."

THE AUTO INDUSTRY had a profound effect upon US guitar manufacturers during the 1950s, not least in its ability to enhance the look of an already stylish object with a rich, sparkling paint finish (like this Chevy Bel Air, right). Gretsch was among the first of the guitar makers to use Du Pont paints – the biggest supplier of paint to the automobile factories – to create instruments such as the 'Cadillac green' Country Club and 'Jaguar tan' Streamliner in 1954. Fender started making the occasional colored guitar at this time, and from 1956 offered the option of 'player's choice' colors, renamed 'custom colors' the following year and including blonde as well as fiesta red.

CHEVROLET
1955

CHEVROLET

PRODUCT VAN
GENERAL MOTORS

▽ FENDER STRATOCASTER
Produced 1954-current; this example 1957

Another rare non-standard colored guitar, this instrument has a beautiful gold finish that accentuates the Stratocaster's flowing curves. The effect is further enhanced by the gold-plated hardware, which, together with the instrument's superb condition, make it a desirable and eminently collectible guitar.

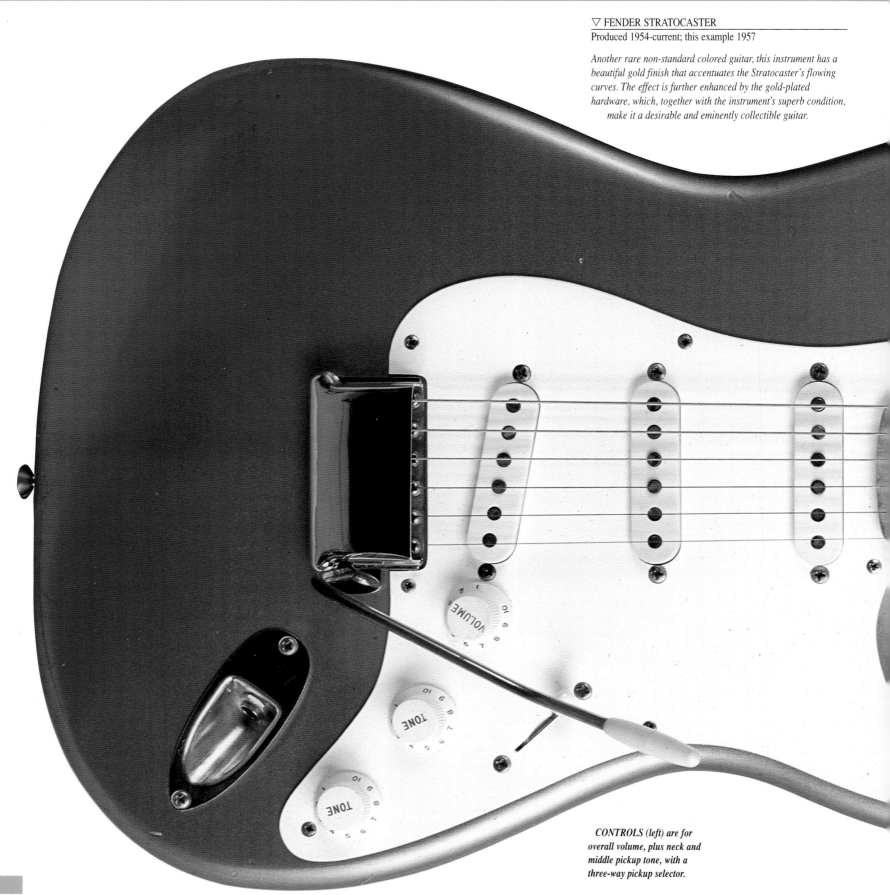

CONTROLS (left) are for overall volume, plus neck and middle pickup tone, with a three-way pickup selector.

1952, and Chet Atkins, probably the best known country guitarist in the world, signed with Gretsch during 1954.

Fender's revenge, so to speak, would come in 1957, with the emergence of Buddy Holly. Holly played a Fender Stratocaster. Granted, Holly could not match the guitar work of Scotty Moore with Elvis, Danny Cedrone with Bill Haley, or Chuck Berry — all of whom played hollowbody Gibsons — but any beginner guitarist could play the sort of fast-strummed chord technique that passed for a guitar solo on Holly's hit 'Peggy Sue'. To a fledgling guitarist, the key to Holly's success was the bright, clear tone of his guitar, not to mention its modern, curvy look. The message was implicit: with a Stratocaster, you don't have to be a great player to sound like a star.

Despite Strat sales in the jillions, Don Randall could not rest easy. "We were always concerned," he says. "We wondered how long this guitar thing would go on. We didn't have any background for it. We had seen the steel guitar, with the huge studios that existed — some of those

AN ENDURING and classic piece of 1950s design, the Stratocaster has a beautifully proportioned body (left) with flowing, sensual curves that created a startling departure from traditional guitar forms.

Jimmy Bryant's influence was helpful in establishing Fender in the West Coast country music community (a tradition carried on by Buck Owens and Merle Haggard), but Bryant, who never had a chart hit in his own right and never had his name on a Fender model, was no match for the big-name endorsers with whom the major makers retaliated: Les Paul, the most successful and popular guitar player of the era, signed with Gibson in

TWENTY-ONE frets (below) remained the standard on the Strat until the mid-1980s.

THE STRAT's neck is fixed to the body at the rear with four screws (usually called bolts).

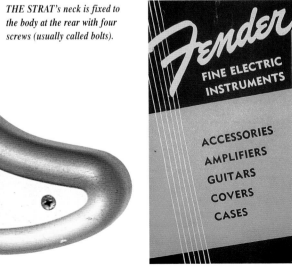

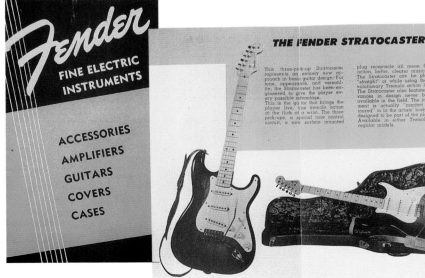

COUNTRY GUITARS *by Thomas Goldsmith*

Country & Western music came to a crossroads in the 1950s. One way led to its old home of Nashville, Tennessee, where the round, warm tones of hollow-body electric guitars snuggled up to an increasingly pop-oriented sound. But at the end of the decade, over in California, the new twangy guitar-based Bakersfield sound took hold as players like Buck Owens & His Buckaroos began to draw the trebliest sounds yet from piercing, solidbody guitars.

ERNEST TUBB & His Texas Troubadours (above) helped the electric guitar gain ground in the conservative musical environment of Nashville in the early 1950s.

COUNTRY GUITARS

As the 1950s dawned, the electric guitar had for only a few years been allowed on the hallowed Grand Ole Opry stage, center of the country music universe. Harold Bradley, one of the finest players of the era, and today president of the Nashville musicians' union, recalls: "The first guy they let play electric guitar on the Opry on a regular basis was Jimmy Short, with Ernest Tubb. Ernest had a hit with electric guitar on it and he would only come on the Opry if they let him bring the electric guitar."

A lean Texan with a homespun baritone that spoke of Western days and honky-tonk nights, Tubb had enjoyed a breakthrough record with 'Walking the Floor Over You', recorded in Dallas in 1941. Its single-noted melodic solo by Fay Smith, probably on a flat-top with a pickup attached to the soundhole, established the electric guitar at the center of Tubb's many subsequent hits. Bradley went on to carry that particular torch in the year that Tubb joined the Opry, as he explains: "In 1943, I played the electric guitar behind Ernest Tubb. I traveled on the road with him between my

junior and senior year in high school. I would play on a Gibson ES-150 with the old bar pickup," he says.

Bradley's use of a hollow-body Gibson with the famous 'Charlie Christian' pickup came out of his jazz orientation, something he shared with many of country's early electric players. Billy Byrd: "My first love when I was growing up was jazz, and I loved the big bands. There wasn't too many places in Nashville and around Middle Tennessee that played a lot of jazz.

"I had a family and I had three little girls," Byrd continues. "I had to stop playing for the kicks and I had to start playing commercial. When I went to work with Ernest in '49, it took me about two years of playing with him to feel free, because I would put a little jazz in there and it wouldn't fit. With Ernest you had to play a certain way or it wasn't Ernest Tubb."

Tubb rewarded Byrd by making him one of the best known guitarists in America, simply by calling: "Take it away, Billy Byrd!" before many of the solos. Byrd's appearances on records, radio and TV went a long way

GRETSCH was noted for finely engraved fingerboard markers (below), influenced by the work of top banjo makers.

FINE MATERIALS were used for the Falcon, such as ebony for the fingerboard (above).

GUITAR CATALOGS were dull and rather reserved until Gretsch's colorful 'Guitars for Moderns' brochure (right) burst on to the scene in 1955.

GUITARS FOR MODERNS BY Gretsch

FRED GRETSCH Jr. (left) had become president of the Fred Gretsch Manufacturing Company in 1948. Gretsch had been established in New York in 1883, but it wasn't until the 1950s that the company's guitars began to make an impact on the market, not least through the series of models bearing the name of top country guitarist Chet Atkins.

Fred Jr. presided over a Brooklyn-based factory that poured out colorful instruments with eye-catching looks and great names. The stunning White Falcon (below) was at the top of the tree, and this together with guitars such as the Country Club, Duo-Jet and Country Gentleman made sure of Gretsch's place in the hall of 1950s guitar fame.

▽ GRETSCH WHITE FALCON
Produced 1955-1980, re-issued 1990; this example 1955

*"Cost was never considered in the planning of this guitar,"
Gretsch boasted of the White Falcon, and at $600 it was by far
the company's most expensive instrument. With a white paint
finish, gold sparkle decorations and gold-plated hardware,
the gleaming Falcon stood out like a beacon against the
relatively drab sunburst and plain natural finishes
of other guitars.*

THE DISTINCTIVE
tailpiece (left) has since been dubbed the 'Cadillac' by collectors because of the resemblance of its 'V' to the automobile company's logo. Also prominent in the metalwork is a 'G' for Gretsch.

FENDER SALES INC., the separate sales company, was still based in Santa Ana – about nine miles south of the Fullerton factory – at the time of this 1956 ad (below). It details that year's principal items in Fender's line of 'fine electric instruments'.

studios had 3000 students. We kind of wondered, knowing the fickleness of the American public, when the organ came along. Maybe they would go back to horns."

Of more immediate concern to Randall was the competition from his fellow guitar makers. Gibson introduced the innovative and successful semi-solidbody model, the ES-335, in 1958; Gretsch dazzled the market with flashy finish colors and ever-more-complicated electronics. Randall kept a close eye on the market and fed information to Leo Fender back in the lab. "Don Randall is the unsung hero of Fender," says Bill Carson. "Leo didn't care until the day he died what was going on up at the sales end. He was always eager to get out two or three new models of amplifiers for a show and maybe one model of guitar," Carson clarifies.

With input from Randall, Fender captured a broader share of the guitar market, with more affordable guitars at the lower end, such as 'three-quarter' size Musicmaster (single pickup) and Duo-Sonic (double pickup) in 1956, and

more refinements on the high end, such as the preset switching capability, 'floating' tremolo (vibrato) and offset body waists of the Jazzmaster in 1958. Still, Randall worried. "All this time I was beating my brains out," he says. "Gibson guitars had been around for 82 years or something [actually since 1902], and everywhere I go I see Gibson guitars, Gibson guitars. Will I ever see anything like this? We did reach the point where we felt like we had our place in the sun, so to speak. I'd say that was somewhere in the 1960s. Through the 1950s it was really a pioneering job."

Fender would continue to prosper in the ensuing decade and, after a stumble under corporate ownership when the company was purchased by CBS in the middle of the 1960s, reach even greater heights as the biggest-selling brandname in the guitar world. Four decades later, virtually all of the company's success would still be based on those pioneering Fender designs of the 1950s, the Telecaster and the Stratocaster. ■ WALTER CARTER

THE SEMI-CIRCULAR walnut 'plug' on the headstock, just above the nut (below right), is evidence of the rear walnut strip, or 'skunk stripe', that covers the channel made to ease insertion of the truss rod into the back of the neck.

IN THE CENTER of the headstock (below) is the 'winged' string guide that replaced the original circular unit around 1956.

Fender STRATOCASTER WITH SYNCHRONIZED TREMOLO   ORIGINAL Contour Body

PRECISION BASS

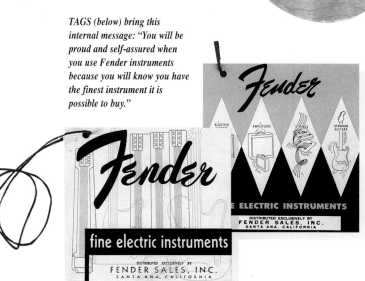

FENDER's 1954 leaflet (left) proudly displays the company's new lineup of three solidbody electric guitars and a lone solidbody bass guitar. The Stratocaster, Telecaster and Esquire are all illustrated with accompanying plush-lined 'Spanish Guitar Cases' that in 1954 would have added an extra $39.95 to the Strat's price of $229.50 (no vibrato) or $249.50 (with vibrato). The Tele was listed at $189.50 and the single-pickup Esquire at $149.50. The Precision Bass ($199.50), which had been launched in 1951, is pictured against the Bassman amplifier.

TAGS (below) bring this internal message: "You will be proud and self-assured when you use Fender instruments because you will know you have the finest instrument it is possible to buy."

Fender fine electric instruments

Fender ELECTRIC INSTRUMENTS

GRADY MARTIN (right) was one of the most prolific and original session guitarists on the Nashville scene, where he started as a teenage fiddler in the 1940s. Through the 1950s he contributed innumerable ground-breaking licks, solos and arrangements, from a lively twin-guitar sound with Jabbo Arrington on early Jimmy Dickens hits such as 'Sleepin

At The Foot Of The Bed' to the twanging bass lines of Johnny Horton and the vinyl-searing 'Knee Deep In The Blues' by Marty Robbins. His other work for Robbins ranged from the proto-fuzz of 'Don't Worry About Me' to the dancing Spanish figures of 'El Paso', and Martin's innovative playing was all over the enduring hits of Patsy Cline.

GRADY MARTIN

in establishing the relatively new image of the stand-up, hot guitar man.

But country guitar and electricity go back much further than the 1950s. In 1934 steel guitarist Bob Dunn attached a pickup to a Mexican guitar and started cranking out imaginative and bluesy solos through a rigged-up amplifier. Dunn's role with Western swing pioneer Milton Brown and his Musical Brownies was echoed in Bob Wills' band a year later by a similarly electrified Leon McAuliffe. Country/swing historian Bob Pinson points to San Antonio's Jim Boyd as the first player to record using an electrified Spanish guitar, in a 1935 session with Roy Newman and his band. Then, in 1937, a stunningly adept, jazz-drenched Eldon Shamblin joined Wills on lead guitar, moving within a few years to early use of the Gibson ES-150

HANK GARLAND (above) won fame with his playing on Red Foley's 1950 'Sugarfoot Rag'. He played many sessions, and crafted memorable guitar duet lines with Chet Atkins for Everly Brothers tunes like 'All I Have To Do Is Dream'. His career was cut short by a car wreck in 1961.

before adopting the electrified Super 400. The marriage of Western fiddle and improvised swing was itself electric, with the amplified instruments giving a country-based style for the first time an ability to compete amid the dim lights and thick smoke of the burgeoning honky-tonk scene.

With the electric guitar firmly established in mainstream country by Tubb, it started showing up everywhere. On the West Coast, with its own thriving country scene, electric guitar was primed to explode because of the innovations of Paul Bigsby and Leo Fender. Even though high-profile players like Byrd and Grady Martin played Bigsbys early on, a general division that would last for years was in the making: round warm tones from the hollow-body guitars of Nashville and trebly twang from the solids of California. "I don't remember the Tele being used much at the Opry," recalls Bradley, a Fender endorser by the 1960s. "I tried it and I couldn't stand it; I had one and I got rid of it. You had to learn to love it and play it and get used to the tone of it."

The players who shaped country guitar for most of the 1950s were in Nashville. Chet Atkins was the best known; he spent ten years at radio and road work before coming to stay at the Opry with the Carter Family in the late 1940s, and shows up playing graceful accompaniment on Carters' tunes like '(This Is) Someone's Last Day'. With a grounding in pop, jazz and blues as well as in country, the precise, innovative Atkins became immeasurably far-reaching, first as a player. His highly developed finger-stylings have made his influence felt from the 1940s to the present day on players as diverse as George Harrison and Lenny Breau. Atkins' careers as producer, solo artist and record company executive helped insure the role of guitar on Music Row throughout the decade and beyond. Nashville's top guitar

ROSA PARKS, a black bus-passenger in Montgomery, Alabama, defies a segregated seating rule when she refuses to give up her seat to a white person. Martin Luther King organizes the year-long Montgomery bus boycott, which leads to the nullification of the bus-segregation laws, and establishes King as leader of the US civil rights movement.

JAMES DEAN is killed in a car wreck; he had earlier in the year appeared in 'chicken run' smash scenes in Rebel Without A Cause. Meanwhile, a disaster at the Le Mans road race in France kills 82 onlookers.

DISNEYLAND is opened in Anaheim, Los Angeles. Walt Disney originally planned to call it 'Mickey Mouse Park'.

PHIL SILVERS debuts on US TV as Sgt. Bilko. A commercial second station, ITA, starts broadcasting in the UK.

CHARLIE PARKER and Albert Einstein die. Einstein's "famous equation linking mass and energy pointed the way to the fission of uranium, and so to Hiroshima and Nagasaki," says a newspaper obituary.

CHUCK BERRY and Bo Diddley cut their debut records (on Chess and Checker). Bill Haley's 'Rock Around The Clock' is number one in the US and UK after it is featured in the movie Blackboard Jungle.

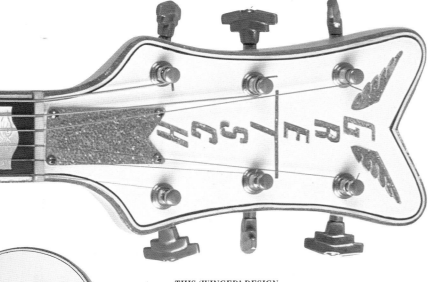

THIS 'WINGED' DESIGN headstock (above) was used by Gretsch only for the White Falcon and White Penguin.

FANCY TUNERS (below right) used on the Penguin and Falcon were Imperial models made by Grover of New York.

△ GRETSCH WHITE PENGUIN
Produced 1956-c1961; this example 1956

Launched at the 1956 National Association of Music Merchants trade show, the White Penguin was a solidbody-style companion to Gretsch's White Falcon. But the Penguin failed to take off, very few were made, and it is now a valuable collectors' item.

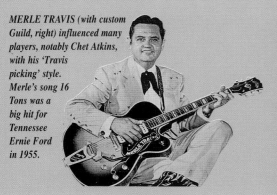

MERLE TRAVIS (with custom Guild, right) influenced many players, notably Chet Atkins, with his 'Travis picking' style. Merle's song 16 Tons was a big hit for Tennessee Ernie Ford in 1955.

JIMMY BRYANT (with Stratosphere Twin, left) came to fame during the early 1950s playing ultra-hot electric guitar solos on Cliffie Stone's Hometown Jamboree TV show in California, working with pedal-steel man Speedy West as The Flaming Guitars. Bryant was one of the first players to use Fender's Broadcaster solidbody, later experimenting with the unusual Stratosphere.

SPEEDY WEST and Jimmy Bryant recorded together; the 'take off' noted on the label of this 45 (above) meant a solo.

guns were friends as well as colleagues, as Byrd recalls: "I used to grab a rhythm guitar and Grady would grab a bass and we would back Chet up." The players' kinship and premium on creativity were at the heart of the Nashville studio approach, where players came up with their own arrangements instead of using standard notation. Their acquaintance with other styles gave an immediacy and accessibility to the country field. But as the 1950s progressed, too much pop perfection drained off some of country's lively, distinctive character in the name of going uptown.

One listen to former country picker Scotty Moore burning down an Elvis Presley side produced in Nashville in 1956 shows that the center of the guitar universe had swiftly shifted away from the Grand Ole Opry. Moore's playing on 'Hound Dog' is sinister and violent, a glimpse into the void

THE BODY (below) is made from sap gum, an unusual choice for guitar building.

STRATOSPHERE's Twin (below) can hardly be said to have the flowing body lines of a Stratocaster, or the traditional reassurance of a Gibson Les Paul.

CONTROLS include two neck selector switches (between the two sets of strings), a three-way pickup selector for the six-string neck, and two on/off switches for the 12-string pickups alongside the volume and tone knobs for each neck.

both during his solos and the fiercely rumbling 16ths he plays under Presley's vocal. You can even hear Moore making mistakes in 'Hound Dog' – and they work.

The youthful Fender company was building its name slowly, long-time Fender associate Bill Carson remembers: "There wasn't very many players on the West Coast. The best one that we had for Telecasters was Jimmy Bryant; he did a lot of albums with Speedy West." Bryant, playing an early Telecaster by 1950, was the ultimate California twangster, playing revolutionary, mile-a-minute stuff that went a long way towards getting the Fender name out front. Carson, himself a Western swing guitarist, worked with the company

getting players and clubs to try amps and guitars; Hank Thompson and Spade Cooley were early endorsers.

Fender had limited success attracting Nashville players to the Tele, but did snag an important one from Memphis, Carson says. "There was one guy that Leo [Fender] thought a lot of and that was Luther Perkins – he exposed the Telecaster to a lot of the audiences when he was playing with Johnny Cash."

Carson says he was also closely involved in developing the contour lines and other features of the Stratocaster. The Strat's capability of bending notes with a vibrato arm, he remembers, came about because steel players were in short supply on the West Coast. Revered Western swing guitarist Eldon Shamblin, who'd joined Bob Wills in 1937, got a special presentation from Leo Fender in 1954. "Eldon had the first experimental finish on a Stratocaster, a gold guitar," Carson says. "Leo gave it to Eldon himself and asked him to try it out. Eldon Shamblin has probably exposed the Stratocaster to more multitudes than anyone else, all the years he's been playing."

But the act that defined the Tele as the ultimate West Coast guitar was Buck Owens and the Buckaroos. Owens had come up with a treble-heavy sound on the low strings while pounding it out in the Bakersfield clubs. "When you're playing a honky-tonk – I played seven years in the

same one called the Blackboard – the bass strings in those days with the old amplifiers would get kind of lost, so I played with a lot of treble," Owens says.

Fender presented Owens and bandmates Don Rich and Doyle Holly with matching bound Telecasters and a Precision bass around 1959, all with an experimental sparkle finish made of ground glass and epoxy. "Leo was always a sucker for a country music band," says Carson. With major stardom for Owens close at hand by the end of the 1950s, he and Rich were about to return Leo Fender's favor by becoming two of the highest profile Telecaster blasters around. "There ain't nothing in this closet but twang," Owens says. "Don't play me nothing that ain't got no twang to it."

Harold Bradley, who spent the decade as a studio star of the first magnitude, is not the only player who well remembers the guitar-driven sound of country from those years. A host of current records, within and without country, echo the creative licks of the Nashville Sound and the energized, treble-happy sound of original West Coast country. In the end, the great country stars of the 1950s built much of their appeal on the creative use of electric instruments, and the relatively new field of electric guitar earned much of its early fame from the hot pickers of Nashville, Bakersfield and beyond. ■ THOMAS GOLDSMITH

NECKS (below) are of one-piece maple, and are bolted Fender-style to the body.

STRATOSPHERE said these standard necks could be replaced by bass or steel necks.

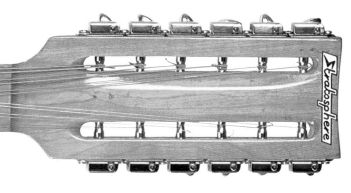

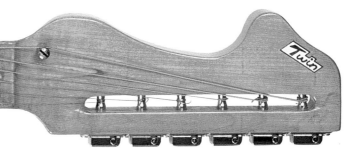

△ STRATOSPHERE TWIN
Produced c1955-1956; this example c1955

"The only twin-necked standard guitar on the market today," boasted the Stratosphere company of Springfield, Missouri, about its astonishing $330 six- and 12-string solidbody instrument – and with the exception of an earlier custom-built twin-neck or two made by Paul Bigsby in California, the claim was correct.

STRATOSPHERE also offered a single-neck guitar in six-string and 12-string versions. As the first company to market an electric 12-string (single- or twin-neck) it had to invent a

tuning for the new instrument. One suggestion paired the doubled strings a musical third apart, rather than today's octave/unison mix, giving a novel twin-guitar sound.

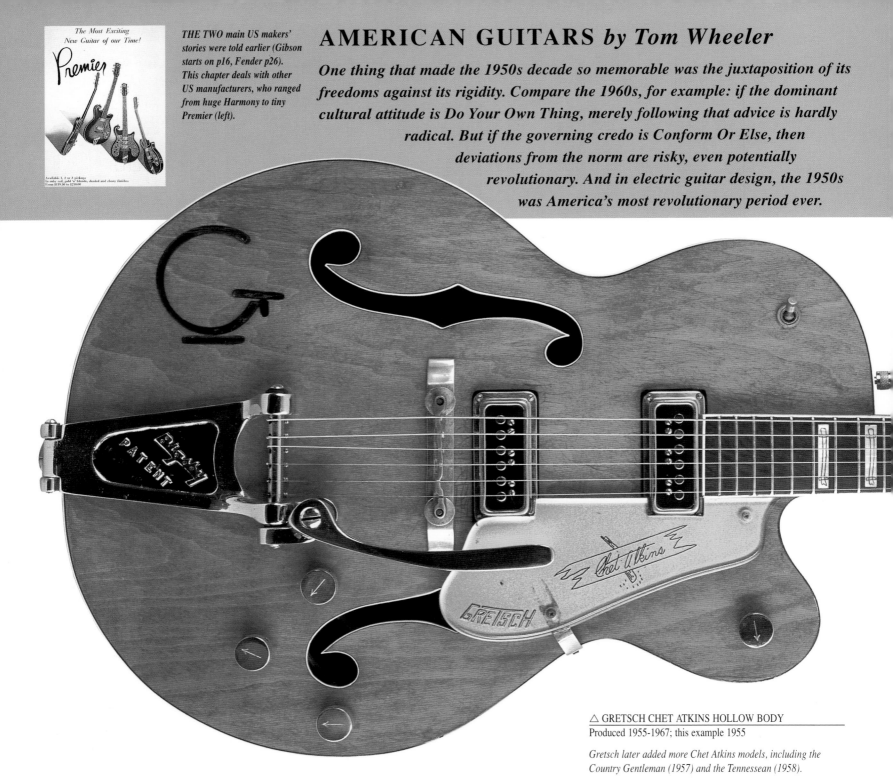

AMERICAN GUITARS *by Tom Wheeler*

One thing that made the 1950s decade so memorable was the juxtaposition of its freedoms against its rigidity. Compare the 1960s, for example: if the dominant cultural attitude is Do Your Own Thing, merely following that advice is hardly radical. But if the governing credo is Conform Or Else, then deviations from the norm are risky, even potentially revolutionary. And in electric guitar design, the 1950s was America's most revolutionary period ever.

△ GRETSCH CHET ATKINS HOLLOW BODY
Produced 1955-1967; this example 1955

Gretsch later added more Chet Atkins models, including the Country Gentleman (1957) and the Tennessean (1958).

AMERICAN GUITARS

The 1950s left us with countless icons, from Coca-Cola bottles and capri pants to transistor radios and tailfins. One of my favorites is the boomerang-shaped ashtray in, say, tangerine. Its separation of form and function is so cavalier, so who-gives-a-damn, it perfectly typifies the playfulness in design that helped energize the period. It was a time when art seemed important enough to integrate into everyday products, when the squiggle-line influences of modernists like Kandinsky and Miró were seen everywhere: Formica counter tops, rec-room curtains, luncheonette menus, you name it. Almost as common were sketches of Our Friend, Mister Atom (nuclear particles apparently look like orbiting planets).

But there was more to 1950s design than amoeba-shaped coffee tables. While the wacky exuberance may have reflected an optimistic embrace of Sputnik-era technology, it co-existed with long-entrenched commitments to no-nonsense practicality. Handy-dandy

time-saver convenience was something of a marketing religion, as was affordability. Manufacturers responded with an assembly-line approach to everything from Tupperware to tract homes (think of those geometric Life magazine aerial photos of prefab subdivisions). Without this crank-'em-out mentality, the economic phenomenon of 'the American Dream' never would have materialized.

So the 1950s saw a contrasting mix of giddy art for the fun of it, rock-ribbed functionality, and an On To The Future optimism ("The Forward Look" as Chrysler called it), all of which made for a charged and challenging musical marketplace. To varying degrees, manufacturers rose to the occasion. Some of their products were wonderful, some were goofy, some were both.

Take Gretsch. Although the company perfectly captured 1950s kitsch futurism with its stereo pickup description, 'Project-O-Sonic', its quirkiest ideas (snap-on back pads, unnecessary string mutes, semi-comprehensible circuits) were actually brainstorms of the following decade. Where I

came from, Gretsches of the 1950s were considered superior to practically all other guitars, something to which you might graduate after, say, an ES-350. That might surprise Gibson aficionados, but I was living in the US South at the time, and Gretsch was endorsed by Chet Atkins himself, and well, that was all anybody needed to know. These guitars were quintessential examples of thoughtfully designed and finely crafted instruments whose features would appeal to any thoroughly modern 'billy: Dynasonic or Filter'Tron pickups, Space Control bridge, StaTite tuners, and finishes more at home on flashy ragtops than flamey archtops.

Gretsch labored to dazzle its customers but also to serve their needs. As the 1950s progressed, lovely and modest designs like the '51 Electro II and Art Deco masterpieces like the cat's-eye Synchromatics gave way to more extravagant creations, but even the late-1950s showboats were unflinchingly touted as guitars of the highest quality. The high-tack, gold-sparkle-trimmed White Falcon may be

CHET ATKINS *put the stamp of approval on Gretsch guitars with an endorsement deal that started in the mid-1950s, and while Nashville's pre-eminent picker may have promoted the Solid Body model, he actually played the Hollow Body.*

△ GRETSCH CHET ATKINS SOLID BODY
Produced 1955-1962; this example 1956

This was in effect Gretsch's earlier Round-Up guitar but with a Bigsby vibrato replacing the earlier instrument's belt-buckle tailpiece. Despite its name, the Solid Body was actually 'semi-solid', with several routed control channels and pockets inside.

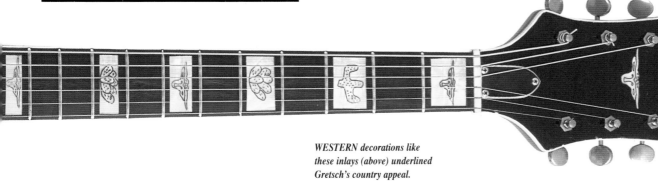

ATKINS himself disliked the unrelenting cowboy trimmings such as the steer's head (left) and the body's 'G-brand', and gradually these were removed or toned down by Gretsch.

WESTERN decorations like these inlays (above) underlined Gretsch's country appeal.

HARMONY was at America's instrument manufacturing hub, which for decades had been Chicago. A report on the company's 60th anniversary in 1952 noted that it produced "more than half of all the fretted instruments made in the US". Harmony made a few

admirable models of professional caliber, as well as huge quantities of moderately priced instruments that found their way into the hands of countless beginners.

HARMONY was in something of a transition during the 1950s between its pre-war success, which was substantial, and its mid-1960s success, which was staggering. Aside from building guitars for mail-order operations such as Sears, Harmony offered everything from bargain flat-tops with stenciled cowboy paintings to electric archtops (as in this ad, left) and nifty little Stratotones.

the most outlandish instrument ever produced in quantity, the guitar's all-time Jayne Mansfield va-va-voom eyepopper, but Gretsch called it simply the best guitar ever, and they meant it. Another example of unapologetically over-the-top styling was the Chet Atkins Solid Body; with its longhorn logo, cows'n'cactus inlays and tooled leather trim, it was a Cadillac cowpoke's yee-haw vision come to earth.

Speaking of blending tradition, art, and The Forward Look: to gaze upon the Rickenbacker line from the 1950s was to see design aesthetics of every decade from the 1930s onwards rolled up into one grand parade. A hint of the Old World was found in Roger Rossmeisl's exquisite raised-ridge (or German Carve) top contouring. America's Depression-era industrial past was echoed in Rickenbacker's 1930s-style Frying Pan lap steel guitars, gigantic horseshoe-magnet pickups, tailpieces that looked like stamped metal, and Doc Kauffman-designed vibratos with fragile housings and exposed springs

plays *Hofner*

UK GUITAR
STAR Bert Weedon
(above) plugs a hollow-
body Hofner Club 50 electric.

Club 40

Club 50

ACOUSTIC/ELECTRIC MODELS

COMMITTEE ELECTRIC
Same specification as the famous Committee Model with the addition of two Hofner high sensitivity pick-ups, two tone controls, two volume controls, and on/off switches.
No. 395 Committee, blonde   75 gns.   No. 396 Committee, brunette   75 gns.

PRESIDENT ELECTRIC
Same specification as the President model with the addition of two Hofner high sensitivity pick-ups, two tone controls, two volume controls and on/off switches.
No. 385 President, blonde   50 gns.   No. 386 President, brunette   50 gns.

SENATOR ELECTRIC
Same specification as Senator model with the addition of one Hofner high sensitivity pick-up, tone and volume controls.
No. 387 Senator, blonde   30 gns.
No. 388 Senator, brunette   30 gns.

*HOFNER in Germany started
making guitars in the 1920s,
with electrics following in the
1950s. A special line was made
from 1953 to be sold in the UK
by Selmer, later including the
small Clubs (far left) and the
larger-body Committee,
President and Senator (left).*

Hofner

*DESPITE the lack of f-holes and
general look, the Club models
came with hollow bodies, making
them comfortably
lightweight.*

*HOFNER's Club 50 (above)
was a cheap two-pickup
hollow-body electric without f-
holes. Along with the one-*

*pickup
Club 40 it saw great service on
the UK beat scene of the late
1950s; a young John Lennon*

(though less awesome than Doc's positively kinky motorized whammy, the standard vibratos were nonetheless idiosyncratic).

These plain Jane utilitarian items were mixed with a fabulous array of mechanical innovations and high-stylin' details – nameplates that looked like the one-piece chrome logos on cars; swept-wing bodies with scimitar soundholes, split-level pickguards, and whopper kitchen-oven knobs; laser-slim necks with double truss rods, triangle markers, and high-gloss fingerboards.

Several of Kay's guitars were well-made and boasted quality features like solid spruce tops, Melita bridges, and Grover Imperial tuners, and the backbone of the line was a series of reasonably good and very affordable guitars in many styles. Still, the company is best remembered for the stylistic boldness of selected models. Take the Barney Kessel's 'Kelvinator' headstock, so nicknamed because of

its heavy Kitchen Of The Future appliance vibe. Its mix of Atomic Age and Art Deco (Atomic Deco!), its lunch-counter gold dots on white plastic, the oversized V that would look right at home on an El Dorado landrocket – has there ever been a more evocative 1950s guitar icon?

An essential principle of Edsel-era guitar chic was that although expensive models were OK, an instrument didn't have to be costly to be cool. To wit: Danelectro. Nat Daniel founded his New Jersey company in 1946 and later cranked out thousands of guitars under the Silvertone (for Sears), Coral, and Danelectro brands. Many had Masonite tops and backs affixed to an interior skeleton of pine, as well as pickup casings made from lipstick tubes. These inexpensive but effective construction methods enabled the guitars produced by the Danelectro company to embody one of American commerce's most esteemed values: they were cheap, but they did the job.

But not all companies leapt into assembly-line production methods, Atomic Deco styling, or gonzo gizmo-mania. Some were concerned more with preserving traditions than breaking new ground. Epiphone's roots went back to the 1870s. By the 1930s it had as good a reputation as any maker in the world, and it extended several of its classic designs from the 1930s and 1940s into the 1950s. Although Gibson purchased the company in '57, the instruments of both incarnations of Epiphone were revered for their style, elegance, and artistry. The electric versions of its flagship, the Emperor, rivaled the best of Gibson, D'Angelico and Stromberg, and its early Sheraton was certainly one of the most distinctive and loveliest thin-bodies ever, with its faceted knobs, yellow pickup housings and Frequensator tailpiece.

Although Guild was founded in 1952 and did introduce some interesting innovations, it was concerned mostly

Guitarist Bert Weedon (l.) checks over final details before recording his first solo sides for Parlophone on Wednesday watched by Sidney Torch (r.), whose orchestra accompanied him, and A&R chief George Martin.

BERT WEEDON was the busiest UK session guitarist in the 1950s. He worked backing visiting stars like Frank Sinatra and Judy Garland, and in the studio helped create British rock'n'roll with acts such as Billy Fury and Tommy Steele. Despite starting his career with an English Abbot-Victor guitar, Weedon moved to Hofner, at first electrifying an archtop acoustic Committee (far left). In 1955 he started a solo career, overseen by A&R man George Martin (center, left) who years later would achieve fame as the Beatles' producer. Weedon had his first hit in 1959 with 'Guitar Boogie Shuffle', a cover version of The Virtues' electric arrangement of Arthur Smith's late-1940s 'Guitar Boogie' instrumental.

▽ HOFNER CLUB 50
Produced 1955-1963; this example c1956

Hofner's Club 40 and Club 50 first appeared in 1955 as part of a UK-only line. Early examples have black-covered pickups and a distinctive oval panel; by 1958 the Clubs had a new rectangular 'flick action' control plate, and soon after adopted more conventional-looking metal-covered pickups. The better quality Club 60 model was added in 1958, at which time the Club 40 was priced at $43, the Club 50 was $52 and the Club 60 cost $66.

▽ SUPRO BELMONT
Produced 1955-1964; this example c1958

Never short of a snappy name, Valco dubbed the Supro Belmont's wild plastic covering the "No-Mar finish", and even managed to refer to the $99.50 guitar's plain ol' pickup as "the clean, clear-toned Melody Unit".

SUPRO (1959 catalog, above) was one of the brandnames used by Valco, who also produced National guitars in the 1950s.

with traditional designs and built some of the decade's most stately and beautiful electric archtops. Several workers were former Epiphone employees, and their old company's heritage was recalled in pearl fingerboard blocks with abalone wedges, or in the Stratford 350's six-button tone selector panel, inspired by the Emperor. Other distinctive Guild touches included white plastic pickup covers and the lovely harp tailpiece.

National and Dobro introduced their most important designs in the 1920s and 1930s, and their post-war successor, Valco, made its biggest splash in the early 1960s. During the 1950s, though, Valco also made a variety of moderately priced electrics, some patterned after the Les Paul and some with bodies actually supplied by Gibson. For players not ready to spring for an ES-175, a Tele, or a Les Paul, Supro's Dual-Tone or Belmont (made by Valco) and

National's Glenwood, Stylist or Bel-Aire were fun and functional alternatives.

Of course, these are just a few of the decade's significant names, spotlighted here because they typified essential aspects of 1950s design. There were others, to be sure, like Paul Bigsby, whose instruments were historically important but very scarce and whose 'company' was a one-man operation; Mosrite, which started in the 1950s but was very much a 1960s phenomenon; and Carvin, a maker of terrific mail-order bargains even back in the 'I Like Ike, I Love Lucy' era.

Well, there's no single guitar that captures the spirit of the time. For me, the period's defining characteristic is its Danelectro-to-D'Angelico diversity, the clashing styles and personalities bumping up against each other like a tangerine boomerang ashtray sitting on a stately old rolltop desk. One thing those designers had in common, though,

was their foresight. After all, they were the ones who perfected the electric guitar's essential aspects. Players with a reverence for vintage instruments or simply an itch for kitsch can find faithful reissues of various models. But even aside from the re-creations, most guitars today borrow heavily from the 1950s pioneers.

Whether they were making double-neck rock-a-hula Rickenbacker lap steels, swingin' Epiphones with cloud markers and vine inlays, or Kay Old Kraftsman 'Jimmy Reed' twang buckets, the 1950s designers were certainly bold. By comparison, the faceless corporate committees responsible for many later innovations seemed timid. They'd never put a big honkin' G cattle brand right on top of a flame-maple guitar. But back in the Project-O-Sonic 1950s, designers weren't burdened by self-consciousness. They experimented, they took risks, they had fun. In other words, they had Style. ■ TOM WHEELER

ROCK'N'ROLL GUITARS *by Rikky Rooksby*

The popularity of the electric guitar was inextricably bound up with the birth in the mid-1950s of rock'n'roll. This was teen music: loud, rhythmic, aggressive, rebellious. And through amplification, the electric guitar could be all these things – as a host of players from Chuck Berry to Bo Diddley set out to prove.

ROCK'N'ROLL GUITARS

Electricity, in the form of pickups and amplifiers, gave the guitar the chance to dominate popular music. Unamplified, it had always been vulnerable to the sheer volume of piano or brass. With amplification, guitarists could play a single note and cut through a band's performance as effectively as the shrillest saxophone.

In most 1950s pop music the guitar had a background role as a chordal instrument, helping to fill out the sound and maybe playing some muted arpeggios – perhaps in a Perry Como or Eddie Fisher hit, for example. But a few talented guitarists like Chet Atkins and Les Paul were able to showcase their abilities and break into the charts.

Guitars like the Gibson Les Paul or the more daring Fender Stratocaster seemed futuristic, giving the

instrument a new-fangled modernity that in many ways is difficult for us to capture now, since these designs are seen today as 'vintage classics'.

When rock'n'roll and rockabilly went mainstream in the mid 1950s, many hit tracks featured electric guitar. Few artists contributed more to the global profile of the guitar than Bill Haley and His Comets. They weren't the best, the rootsiest or the hippest, but they had over a dozen hits in 1955 and 1956 with which to spread the message, and were seen in films like Blackboard Jungle. Often in early

CHUCK BERRY is arguably the most influential rock guitarist of the 1950s. He's seen here in classic 'duck walk'

pose (right) with the Gibson ES-350T on which he brought to life his fresh hybrid of boogie, country and blues.

THE 350T started life with these P90 pickups (left), later gaining humbucker types.

CONTROLS *were standard: a volume knob (front) and tone knob (back) for each pickup.*

GIBSON made fewer natural-finish examples of their archtop models (such as the ES-350T above) than they did sunburst, and collectors today will pay a premium for these rarer

guitars. For example, in 1957 only 43 of the total of 147 ES-350Ts made at Gibson's factory in Kalamazoo, Michigan, had a natural finish to their laminated maple tops.

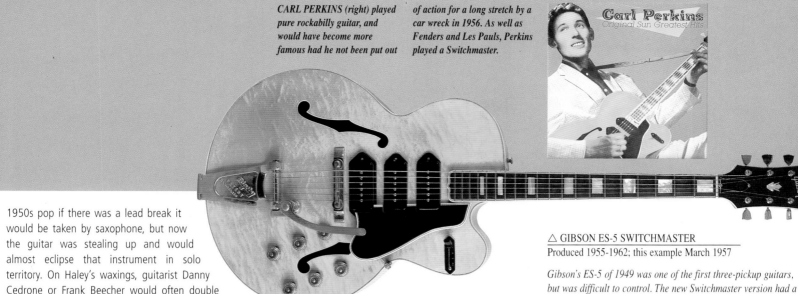

1950s pop if there was a lead break it would be taken by saxophone, but now the guitar was stealing up and would almost eclipse that instrument in solo territory. On Haley's waxings, guitarist Danny Cedrone or Frank Beecher would often double the saxophone, sometimes (as on 'Mambo Rock', recorded in 1955) harmonizing a musical third above. Songs like 'Rock Around The Clock' (the recorded solo of which was played by an apparently country-influenced Cedrone), 'Rock The Joint', 'Shake, Rattle and Roll', and 'Razzle-Dazzle' had short but attention-grabbing guitar solos, and the playing is often quite fast for the time.

There's no doubt that Scotty Moore, who recorded with Elvis Presley throughout the decade, is another key figure. Presley's worldwide audience may not have known Moore by name, but the solos on early Sun tracks such as 'That's Alright' and on the RCA sides 'Heartbreak Hotel', 'Hound Dog' and 'Blue Suede Shoes' contributed much to the excitement of those cuts. And Moore, who was also Presley's original manager, usually didn't have to compete with a saxophonist. On 'My Baby Left Me' Moore's deft

picking comes through, and the guitar on 'Heartbreak Hotel' certainly holds its own with the tinkling piano. Moore's elegant and adaptable style owed something to the flatpicking of Les Paul and Tal Farlow and the fingerpicking of Merle Travis and Chet Atkins.

Moore's churning solo on 'Too Much' (recorded 1956) is infamous as one of the more anarchic moments in 1950s rock guitar, but as with other rock players of the era his breaks are more often based on chords rather than scales, as with the lead in 'Blue Moon of Kentucky', or the fret-shifting 'Good Rockin' Tonight'. On that track Moore also makes use of hitting the open E string against an E of the same pitch on the second string, because the available

string gauges of the 1950s were too heavy to allow players to get such unison effects by bending one of the strings (as they would go on to do in the 1960s).

Sam Phillips had recorded other strong guitar parts at Sun: before Presley and Moore came along there was Junior Parker's proto-rockabilly 45 'Love My Baby' with its blistering solo from guitarist Floyd Murphy. Working at the same time as Presley was Carl Perkins who was influenced by the choppy guitar riffs of T-Bone Walker. Perkins recorded his own song 'Blue Suede Shoes' in 1956 with a Gibson Les Paul, as well as later rockabilly tracks like 'Lend Me Your Comb' and 'Matchbox'. Meanwhile in Capitol's studios in Los Angeles, Cliff Gallup was kicking up

△ GIBSON ES-5 SWITCHMASTER
Produced 1955-1962; this example March 1957

Gibson's ES-5 of 1949 was one of the first three-pickup guitars, but was difficult to control. The new Switchmaster version had a volume and tone control per pickup and a pickup selector switch.

▽ GIBSON ES-350T
Produced 1955-1981; this example January 1957

Gibson launched three guitars during 1955 in their its 'thinline' style, in an attempt to produce more comfortable guitars than its existing deep-bodied electric archtops. The ES-350T (as well as the 225T and Byrdland) had a shallower body (around 2in deep), a shorter string-length and a shorter, narrower neck.

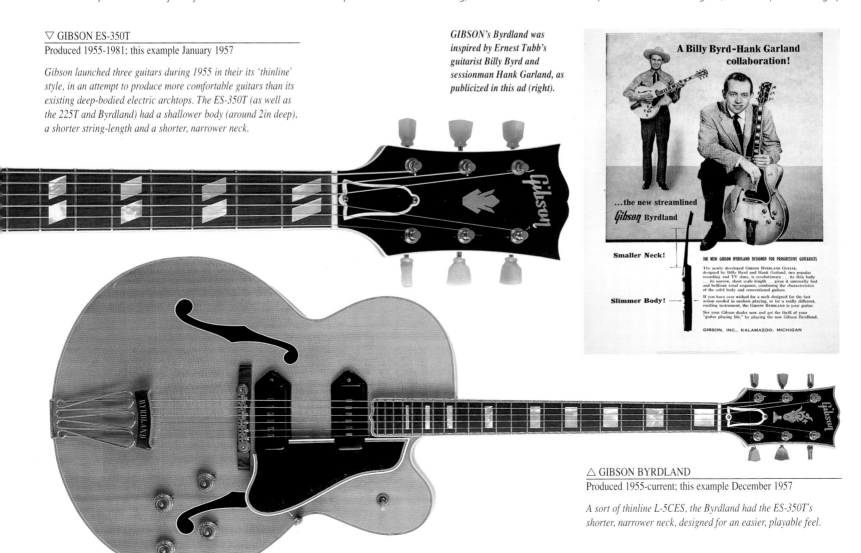

GIBSON's Byrdland was inspired by Ernest Tubb's guitarist Billy Byrd and sessionman Hank Garland, as publicized in this ad (right).

△ GIBSON BYRDLAND
Produced 1955-current; this example December 1957

A sort of thinline L-5CES, the Byrdland had the ES-350T's shorter, narrower neck, designed for an easier, playable feel.

1956

BRIGHT colors became hip in the 1950s, whether on the Technicolor movie screen or in the Formica world of the dream home. As we've seen, guitar makers like Gretsch and Fender quickly exploited this colorful trend. Danelectro's budget-conscious guitars were not far behind, as the New Jersey company's flyer (right) shows with its fuchsias, bronzes, peaches and sands.

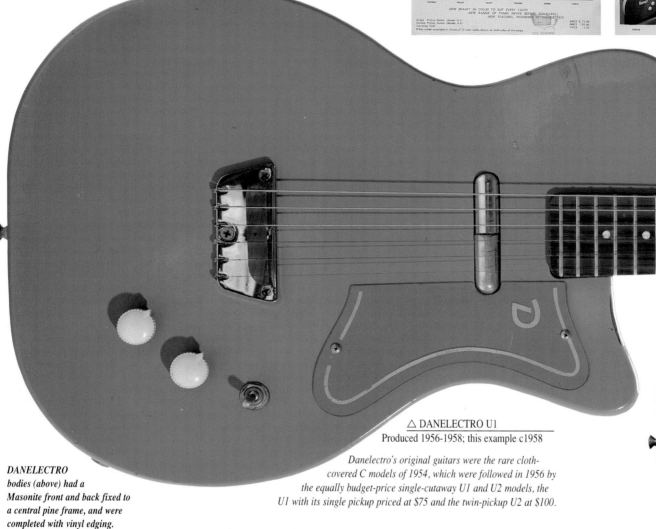

DANELECTRO's idiosyncratic 1950s metal pickup covers (left) were in fact made from lipstick tubes.

DANELECTRO bodies (above) had a Masonite front and back fixed to a central pine frame, and were completed with vinyl edging.

△ DANELECTRO U1
Produced 1956-1958; this example c1958

Danelectro's original guitars were the rare cloth-covered C models of 1954, which were followed in 1956 by the equally budget-price single-cutaway U1 and U2 models, the U1 with its single pickup priced at $75 and the twin-pickup U2 at $100.

---

a storm. Although Gallup's time with Gene Vincent amounted to less than a year, his contribution to 31 Vincent recordings, including the tracks 'Be Bop A Lula', 'Race With The Devil' and 'Bluejean Bop' (1956), is now seen as seminal rockabilly guitar work, and his brilliant cameos at the heart of Vincent's 45s remain perfect lessons in brevity and style. Gallup dropped out of Vincent's band because he disliked touring, but Johnny Meeks stepped into his shoes with considerable aplomb, striding out on tracks such as the riff-laden 'Dance To The Bop' (1957).

In the 1950s one man became synonymous with the electric guitar, not least by writing the most famous song ever about a poor country boy who learns to play, takes his talent to the city and gets his name in lights. The song was 'Johnny B Goode' and the singer was Chuck Berry. By creating this folk hero for the amplified instrument Berry had an incalculable effect in mythologising it. He wrote the rule book for the fast shuffle boogie solo, and had a trademark intro – the guitar taking the first four bars of the twelve, the band coming in on bar five – as can be heard

on 'Roll Over Beethoven' among many, many others. A variant was 'No Particular Place To Go', which commences with Berry tootling an augmented chord, its dissonance mimicking a car horn. The songs had central solos where Berry would play a series of musical fourths, spiced up with 'bent' notes (from blues) and high descending thirds (from country). On 'Johnny B Goode' the guitar contributes

NEARLY FOUR DECADES after their biggest successes in the 1950s, two guitar-toting rock'n'rollers were included in a series of US stamps issued to honor outstanding American

individuals involved in the performing arts. Buddy Holly (above left) did not, of course, survive the 1950s, while Bill Haley (above right) lived until 1981 when he died at age 55.

little interjections, and has almost gained a voice in its own right: Berry had foregrounded the guitar to talk back at him. There's no doubt Berry is the man who more than anyone else 'invented' rock guitar, and his records remain a recurring source of renewal in rock music.

Listening to recorded rock guitar solos of the 1950s, certain typical features emerge. Heavy-gauge strings made string bending difficult, so it is employed more sparingly than it would be by the blues-rock players of the 1960s and 1970s. Semitone bends are therefore more typical, and at the time this toying with the pitch of a note helped to further rock guitar's rebellious image – the subtext being: we're rebels, because we don't care about your notions of what's 'in tune'.

The emphasis in guitar solos of the 1950s tends to be rhythmic rather than melodic or harmonic, again in contrast to lead breaks of later decades. Movement around the neck was limited, and broken chords were the order of the day.

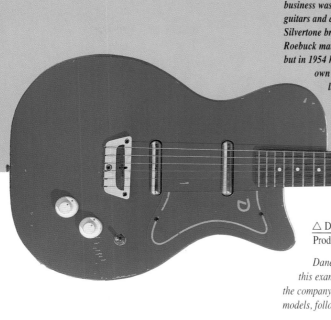

NATHAN DANIEL's main business was the production of guitars and amps with the Silvertone brand for the Sears, Roebuck mail-order company, but in 1954 he began to put his own brand on a similar line of instruments, called Danelectro. The guitars were boldly styled and used inexpensive, basic materials. Daniel and his colleagues came up with a variety of designs based on this cheap and cheerful ethos, including a six-string bass (see p75). Daniel sold his company in 1967 to the MCA music company, which added its record-label name Coral to some of the instruments.

△ DANELECTRO U2
Produced 1956-1958; this example c1958

Danelectro's double-pickup partner to the U1 was the U2, this example finished in a dazzling red lacquer. In late 1958 the company replaced the U line with a series of twin-cutaway models, following the trend away from single-cutaway guitars.

TOPPING Danelectro's bolt-on poplar neck was a distinctive headstock (below right), the shape of which has given rise to the nickname 'Coke bottle' among collectors.

▽ FENDER MUSICMASTER
Produced 1956-1980; this example 1957

Fender's two new 1956 guitars, the Musicmaster and two-pickup Duo-Sonic, had a shorter string-length than usual; the company said they were "ideal for students, and adults with small hands".

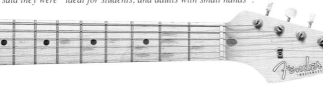

FENDER began a series of ads in the 1950s where an odd scenario is tagged with the phrase 'You Won't Part With Yours Either'; these two (right) feature the Musicmaster.

▽ FENDER DUO-SONIC
Produced 1956-1969, re-issued 1993; this example 1959

Like its single-pickup ally the Musicmaster, the Duo-Sonic too featured an anodized aluminum pickguard during the 1950s.

You won't part with yours either*

You won't part with yours either*

THE FIRST underwater transatlantic telephone cable linking the US and the UK opens for service.

SOUTHDALE CENTER "the world's biggest shopping town" opens in Minneapolis, with 72 stores on a 10-acre site. It becomes the model from which most other malls are cloned.

ROCK Around The Clock becomes a movie and defines the standard rock movie plot about a manager who discovers an unknown group (Haley & His Comets) and hits it big. Meanwhile, Hollywood deals with drug addiction for the first time in Otto Preminger's The Man With The Golden Arm.

THE HUNGARIAN uprising is quelled by invading Soviet tanks as martial law is imposed.

BOXER Rocky Marciano retires undefeated having won every one of his 49 professional fights, all but six by a knockout.

THE BRITISH parliament votes to end the death penalty.

THE SUEZ CRISIS develops when the UK, France and Israel retaliate against Egypt for nationalizing the Suez Canal. Air attacks on Egypt ensue, and the USSR threatens a nuclear response. A ceasefire in November at last calms a tense, fearful world.

BUDDY HOLLY kicked off a 25-date UK tour in 1958 at the Trocadero in London (right) with Joe B Maudlin on bass and Jerry Allison on drums.

The guitar tone was generally clean, although it wasn't too long before players started to experiment with a little distortion. One short echo ('slapback') was popular to thicken the sound.

While Chuck Berry was cutting hits for Chess in Chicago, its sister label Checker was releasing the R&B records of Bo Diddley. Both Diddley and Berry would have a significant later influence on the career of the Rolling Stones. Diddley had nothing like the same commercial impact as Berry, but his forceful rhythm was another advance for the guitar, and he pioneered tremolo and distortion. He was one of the first players to approach the electric guitar as an instrument in its own right, rather than a means of playing acoustic ideas louder.

His 1955 cut 'Bo Diddley', for example, is a thumping monochord of sound, with the guitar just occasionally breaking out from his insistent signature rhythm, while on 'Pretty Thing' from the following year Diddley plays an arresting intro quite different than Chuck Berry's dial-ins, as well as a brief chordal break which sounds like he's imitating the harmonica. 'Bo's Guitar' (1958) is an instrumental that

RICKENBACKER's unusual body shape (below) did not survive the 1950s; it's the company's more elegant designs from later in the decade (see p74) that have come to be considered as Rickenbacker's true classics.

RICKENBACKER's Combos featured anodized metal pickguards (left), as did some Fender guitars in 1956.

reveals a little more of Diddley's tone than most of the early cuts, and he uses lots of strange noises by scraping the lower strings with a pick. In the same year his tremolo'd lower-string riff even gets to lead in the doo-wop 'I'm Sorry', and the break on 'Crackin Up' (1959) is a good example of the chordal nature of much 1950s soloing. The vehicle for Diddley's music was a series of strikingly shaped guitars built by Gretsch.

Mainstream pop continued to have less room for the guitar than rock'n'roll. In a genre like doo-wop, for example, the emphasis was on vocal harmony, and teen ballads needed orchestral arrangements. Although the first wave of rock'n'rollers died – some were burned out, others were jailed, found the Lord, or joined the army – the electric guitar carried on.

The popularity of guitar instrumentals showed that rock'n'roll had put the electric guitar firmly and permanently on the musical map, exemplified by such original cuts as Link Wray & His Ray Men's sinister 'Rumble' (1958), or the more popular work of Duane Eddy whose first hit instrumental, 'Rebel Rouser', came along in 1958 with sax-man Gil Bernal in hot pursuit.

Eddy made his low-pitched guitar melodies into a trademark, sometimes playing them on six-string bass, with lots of reverb and a tremolo unit to help color the sound. Eddy mostly used a Gretsch Chet Atkins Hollow Body because he liked its tone, though he was never completely comfortable with its construction and had to stuff the body to minimize feedback. Meanwhile in Britain Bert Weedon became the first guitarist to break the Top 40,

with 'Guitar Boogie Shuffle' in 1959 (it had been a hit earlier in the year for The Virtues in the US). In 1957 Weedon had put together the 'Play In A Day' teaching book which would have an immense influence in the UK.

The main player associated with the Fender Stratocaster in the 1950s was Buddy Holly. His fast strumming, coupled with the guitar work of Niki Sullivan, was an integral part of their hits. Ricky Nelson's 45s were enlivened by the fluent Telecaster bending of James Burton, and another important player was Eddie Cochran, whose rhythm work on 'Summertime Blues' (1958), 'C'Mon Everybody' and

'Something Else' (1959) was an essential element. Favoring a Gretsch, Cochran could turn in rhythmic Berry-like solos on 'Completely Sweet', use musical thirds in 'Don't Ever Let Me Be', or play typical chordal breaks.

By the end of the 1950s rock'n'roll was ebbing as a commercial force. Many of its leading practitioners were out of action, out of time, or out of luck. But the seeds of rock guitar were planted in a generation who would come through in the 1960s, taking these ideas and playing them through bigger amps at greater volume. The rock'n'roll sound would live on, turned up to 11. ■ RIKKY ROOKSBY

*THE THROUGH-NECK style
has a neck (below) extending the
length of the guitar, and added
'wings' complete the body.*

△ RICKENBACKER COMBO 400
Produced 1956-1958; this example 1956

*The Combo 400 was one of the first Rickenbacker guitars to point
the way toward the success that the company would enjoy in the
next decade. It replaced Rickenbacker's earlier and ungainly
'horseshoe' pickup with a modern-looking unit, and featured a
through-neck construction that was practical and cost-effective.*

*RICKENBACKER was founded
by Swiss immigrant Adolph
Rickenbacker in California in the
1920s, at first as a small tool-and-
die operation. Rickenbacker soon
grabbed guitarists' attention by
introducing one of the first electric
lap-steel guitars of the early
1930s, moving to conventional
electric Spanish guitars after
Adolph sold out to businessman
F.C. Hall in 1953.*

*RICKENBACKER's stylish logo
(above) with its interlinked letters
recalls automobile logos of the
1950s that were designed as one
continuous strip of chrome.*

JAPANESE guitars of the 1950s often muddled the form and function of the American instruments they copied. Guyatone's designers, for instance, made visual allusions to a resonator guitar with the three-pickup EG-300's metal body plates (below), but these were purely decorative.

JAPANESE GUITARS *by Hiroyuki Noguchi*

Despite the fact that a small, modest electric guitar industry had started to grow in Japan following World War II, Japanese guitarists of the 1950s desired nothing less than American instruments upon which to play American-inspired music. Japanese guitar makers learned quickly that they had to export in order to survive.

TOKYO SOUND (catalog, right) was set up by Mitsuo Matsuki in the late 1940s to manufacture Guyatone guitars.

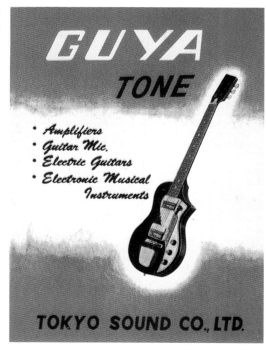

GUYA TONE

• Amplifiers
• Guitar Mic.
• Electric Guitars
• Electronic Musical Instruments

TOKYO SOUND CO., LTD.

JAPANESE GUITARS

Dance halls grew in popularity in mid-1930s Tokyo, with Western-style bands playing jazz, fox trot, tango and Hawaiian music. One such Hawaiian musician on the dance hall scene was guitarist Buckie Shirakata (1912-1994), a second-generation Japanese-American who had arrived at Yokohama port from Hawaii in 1935 with a Rickenbacker 'Frying Pan' guitar. It is said that this was the first electric guitar to be brought into Japan.

At the same time, electric guitars were being developed by the Japanese. As in America, this began with steel guitars. Among those who had heard about the invention of the electric guitar in the US was Atsuo Kaneko (1916-1993), and he began independent research into the making of electric guitars (and would later became one of the founders of the Teisco company). Kaneko loved Hawaiian music and jazz, playing in a Tokyo band. Around

1934, he got to know Mitsuo Matsuki, who owned a hardware store near his home. Matsuki, too, was hooked on Hawaiian music and fascinated by the idea of electric guitars. Kaneko and Matsuki got on very well with one another, and made a couple of prototype electric steel guitars together. Matsuki would later go on to set up the Guyatone company (see top of facing page).

Kaneko continued to play in his band, and developed a prototype electric guitar with Hiroyoshi Hashimoto (born 1915) who in 1948 would join Teisco. Kaneko and Hashimoto performed in various dance halls and small theaters using their own steel guitars and amplifiers, but in October 1940 the authorities forced the closure of dance halls, which they regarded as symbols of frivolity and pleasure. Gradually, it became difficult to perform jazz and Hawaiian music in public places. In December 1941, when war broke out between Japan and the USA, English was

48

GUYATONE's mid-1950s catalog features the EG-300 and an amplifier on the cover.

BUCKY SHIRAKATA (above, second from right) became the first electric guitarist in Japan when in the mid-1930s he imported an electric lap-steel guitar from Hawaii. Here (above) he plays at an event in Tokyo in 1952 to celebrate Gibson's appointment of a Japanese distributor.

▽ GUYATONE EG-300
Produced c1956-1958; this example c1956

Early Japanese makers of electric guitars, such as Guyatone, began to develop hollow-body electrics during the first half of the 1950s, primarily as a reaction to the expensive imported American models that became available at the time. Guyatone's EG-300 model was one of the earliest to reach production.

▽ TEISCO J-1
Produced 1954-c1960; this example c1956

Just as Gibson had the Les Paul and its Junior model, so Teisco had the solidbody Les Paul-inspired TG-54 and its junior version, the J-1, both issued during 1954. The J-1's pickup was also used by Teisco on some steel guitar models.

THE DESIGN of the J-1 is clearly American-inspired, even if Teisco did manage to incorporate one more fret than Gibson's Les Paul Junior.

totally forbidden. There was a military atmosphere everywhere in Japan, and the atmosphere was heightened in January 1943 when the Japanese government announced a ban on Western music, under which overseas music was completely forbidden.

Military defeat in August 1945 turned all the values in Japan completely upside down. Jazz and Hawaiian music, previously banned as enemy music, inundated the radio waves, and people were comforted by bright and cheerful Western music. Even worn-out records or guitars with a few missing strings sold well. The era of oppression had ended and the democratic age had arrived.

Musicians became free too, able to perform their favorite music on their favorite instruments without any restrictions. Demobilized servicemen formed bands and played in clubs built to offer entertainment to the 400,000 occupying troops. In 1946, Atsuo Kaneko returned to

Tokyo and began playing again. He started once more to make pickups and steel guitars, and approached the Fuji Onkyo sound company in Tokyo about producing steel guitars. Kaneko and Dohryu Matsuda (born 1921), an engineer with Fuji Onkyo, collaborated successfully together, and in the summer of 1946 they established the Awoi Sound Research Institute (later renamed Teisco Co. Ltd.) in Minato-ku, Tokyo, with the aim of manufacturing a line of electric guitars and amplifiers.

Guyatone and Awoi (Teisco) were located close to one another in Tokyo, and at first in the 1950s there was contact between the two companies, and probably some influencing of each other's products. Both produced steel guitars, amplifiers, and pickups. Later, when the businesses were in competition, they became rivals.

In the 1950s, thanks to the special procurement orders for the Korean War, Japan saw a remarkable economic

recovery. In 1952, the Peace Treaty and the US/Japan Security Treaty came into effect, putting an end to the occupation. At once there was an unprecedented Western music boom in Japan. Live performances at big theaters played to full houses, and jazz and Hawaiian music gained new popularity, as did country music. Later, rockabilly appeared on the scene, as well as Japanese versions of Elvis Presley and other rock'n'roll acts.

As the 1950s developed, hollow-body electric guitars drew much attention. Every Japanese guitarist aspired to have an f-hole Gibson or Epiphone guitar – and Gibson, for example, appointed a Tokyo-based distributor in 1952. But imported guitars were extremely expensive. Not everybody could afford to buy one. Teisco and Guyatone could see that this style of electric guitar would be in demand and started to develop their own hollow-body electric models. Teisco unveiled the EO-180 in 1952, the EP-6 in 1953 and

1957

▽ GIBSON LES PAUL CUSTOM
Produced 1954-1961, 1968-current; this example 1957

In 1957 Gibson changed the layout of the Les Paul Custom model by installing three new humbucking pickups to replace the previous pair of single-coil types, as well as a modified three-way switch to provide what Gibson described as a "much wider range of tone coloring". Humbucking pickups reduce the hum and electrical interference that can afflict standard single-coil pickups, by wiring two coils together out of phase and with opposite magnetic polarities. Players and collectors especially seek out Gibson's early humbuckers with 'PAF' (patent applied for) labels fixed to the base, used between 1957 and 1962.

CHET ATKINS "COUNTRY GENTLEMAN" GUITAR

This handsome showpiece has slim 17" closed body with simulated inlaid "F" holes. Grover 16-to-1 ratio enclosed gears. Bigsby Tremolo and Tailpiece. Adjustable rod—Actionflo neck. Satin ebony Neo-Classic fingerboard. Heavy 24-karat gold plating and rich mahogany-grained country style finish. Gretsch Filter'Tron twin electronic heads. Trim, fine-quality leather shoulder strap.

PX6122 Chet Atkins "Country Gentleman" Electric Guitar **$575.00**

THIS NEW three-pickup layout (below) was probably prompted by Fender's Strat.

THE THIRD GUITAR in Gretsch's Chet Atkins series, the Country Gentleman (shown in a 1959 catalog, left) was from its launch in 1957 produced with a single-cutaway body. It would move to twin-cutaway style in 1961.

BLOCK fingerboard inlays (above) were always used for the Les Paul Custom model.

SALES hit a peak during 1956 and 1957 of Gibson's Les Paul series, which included six models: the $375 black Custom, by 1957 in revised three-humbucker guise (above); the $247.50 gold-top; the $179.50 beige Special; the $132.50 beige TV; and the $120 sunburst Junior, which was also available at the same price in a 'three-quarter' format with a shorter neck, designed for beginners. Les Paul himself often favored the black

Custom for live work, as he explains: "When you're on stage with a black tuxedo and a black guitar, the people can see your hands move, with a spotlight on them: they'll see your hands flying." Paul was an incorrigible tinkerer, rarely able to leave a guitar the way it came from the factory. The Custom he's seen using in 1957 (right) has had a body built specially for him with the flat, uncarved top he preferred.

the EP-4 and EP-5 in 1955, and Guyatone developed the EG-300 in the early 1950s. Around this time, instrument importers in Western countries became interested in Japanese-made electric guitars. Buyers from the United States placed orders with both Teisco and Guyatone, and exports came to occupy a large part of their business.

Thanks to electric guitars, the position of the guitar in bands was largely improved in 1950s music. However, except for Hawaiian music, guitars rarely played a central role in Japanese bands. It was not until the 1960s, with the popularity of solidbody instruments, that electric guitars took their place at the heart of the music.

During the 1950s Mitsuo Matsuki of Guyatone received a 45 record from an American friend. Matsuki says he doesn't remember the title of the tune, but remembers that it was by Les Paul and Mary Ford. It included a clear guitar sound he had never heard before. He says he was mesmerized by the sound, and that while he realized that it must be an electric guitar, he didn't think it was the sound of a hollow-body instrument. Matsuki says he instinctively felt that it was not a steel guitar, but a guitar with a solid body. This marked the beginning of Matsuki's

CHET ATKINS and Jimmie Webster, Gretsch's main guitar ideas-man, are seen (right) at a trade event in 1958. Atkins holds his new Gretsch signature model, the Country Gentleman, the name of which he says was inspired by the title of one of his records. "When 'Country Gentleman' had been a hit I guess it was probably Gretsch's idea to put out another model. They were selling so many of the orange Chet Atkins they wanted to put out a little more expensive guitar, with good tuning pegs, better wood selection, and a body that was generally larger and thinner." Jimmie Webster, a musician who became responsible for many of Gretsch's guitar designs and novel features, is holding an early version of the company's White Falcon Stereo guitar.

▽ GRETSCH CHET ATKINS COUNTRY GENTLEMAN
Produced 1957-1981; this example 1961

The Country Gent was Gretsch's first guitar with a 'thinline' body, as established by Gibson, and the first with its new Filter'Tron humbucker pickups, devised by engineer Ray Butts and launched in 1957, the same year as Gibson's humbuckers.

GIBSON reserved its fancy split-diamond headstock inlay for top-of-the-line guitars, such as the Les Paul Custom (below), or the Super 400CES (right) that Scotty Moore (far right) is playing with Elvis Presley in a scene from the 1957 movie Jailhouse Rock.

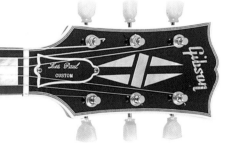

THE SOVIET UNION launches within a month Sputnik I and II, the first artificial satellites to orbit the earth. Sputnik II has a dog, Laika, on board, proving that life can survive in space. A subsequent attempt to launch a satellite by the US in December fails. The space race begins.

IN THE UK, the Wolfenden Report calls for homosexual acts between consenting adults to be decriminalized.

NUCLEAR TESTS in the Pacific are condemned by mass protests in Tokyo, but the demos fail to stop Britain explode its first H-bomb near Christmas Island. Nevil Shute's On The Beach, a horrific vision of worldwide nuclear devastation, is published.

ELVIS PRESLEY stars as Vince Everett in his third film, Jailhouse Rock (poster above, and still above left), with a set of songs 'mostly' composed by Jerry Leiber and Mike Stoller.

RADIO FANS listen to hits such as 'Come Go With Me' (Dell-Vikings), 'Peggy Sue' (Buddy Holly) and 'Bye Bye Love' (Everly Brothers).

TV DEBUTS include Wagon Train, Perry Mason, and Zorro in the US, and Emergency Ward 10, Pinky & Perky, and Six-Five Special in the UK.

JACK KEROUAC launches the Beat Generation with his novel On The Road, as Sal Paradise and Dean Moriarty roam America to a jazz soundtrack.

research into solidbody guitars. After much trial and error, a prototype was completed, and in 1955 a model called the Les Paul Guitar was released on to the market. Into the late 1950s, solidbody guitar models such as the LG line (30, 50 and 60) were developed by Matsuki and Guyatone. These models were primarily intended for export, and some were sold in the UK with brandnames such as Antoria as well as Guyatone.

Teisco's engineers had also seen an early 1950s Gibson Les Paul, which gave them the opportunity to develop a solidbody electric guitar. Noboru Arai, a jazz guitarist and good friend of Hiroyoshi Hashimoto, started to use a Les Paul gold-top around 1953. Hashimoto fell in love with it at first sight. He wanted to make the same guitar, so he borrowed the instrument from Arai.

The engineering team at Teisco thoroughly researched Arai's Gibson, and after great efforts completed their first solidbody electric guitar, the TG-54, in March 1954. Three months later a 'junior' J-1 version was unveiled. Between that time and the end of the decade several more models were developed, and as with Guyatone all were basically intended for export. With the exception of steel guitars,

Japanese guitarists of the 1950s did not use Teisco or Guyatone electric guitars. In Japan at that time everyone had great faith in anything American. Nobody paid much attention to domestic products when American products were of such high quality. Teisco and Guyatone were searching for a major breakthrough, but their products were inferior compared to the instruments that were being produced in the United States at the time.

However, combined with the remarkable expansion of electric guitar exports in the later 1950s, technology advanced and mass-production systems were established. It was not until the mid-1960s that electric guitars became available to the ordinary Japanese, triggered by the sweeping popularity of the instrumental American guitar group The Ventures. Many electric musical instrument companies suddenly appeared, like mushrooms after rain, all trying to follow Teisco and Guyatone. But for Japanese electric guitar manufacturers the 1950s had been a gradual learning period in which they grew in size and strength, making steady progress that would in later decades allow them to catch up with and overtake American guitar makers. ■ HIROYUKI NOGUCHI

MAIL-ORDER GUITARS *by Michael Wright*

CHICAGO-based Kay and Harmony were among the main suppliers of guitars to mail-order companies. Kay's own lines included the high-end Barney Kessel series, previewed by the jazz guitarist in a 1957 ad (left).

For many American guitarists in the 1950s without a fortune to spend on a first instrument, the great mail-order catalogs provided just what was needed... and all delivered directly to your door, whether you were in a big city or stuck out in the middle of nowhere. Best known of all were the basic, affordable Silvertone brand instruments made for the Sears, Roebuck catalog.

ALL THREE of Kay's Barney Kessel models – the Pro, Artist, and Jazz Special – came with options of one or two pickups (below) and in natural or sunburst finish. The Artist and Special had a Melita bridge, as seen on some Gretsch models.

IT'S THE YEAR FOR **K**

AND

KESSEL

KAY

Exit flowery phrases. Enter this simple announcement, yet tinged with deep pride, that Kay and the nation's number one jazz guitarist Barney Kessel—winner of the Down Beat, Metronome, and Playboy polls—have together developed a professional guitar which will establish new standards in quality of sound, workmanship and design.

You are invited to see the gold ribbons untied at the NAMM convention united where Barney himself will play in the 'K' CLUB, *Music House.*

And speaking of 1957,' the Kay's Music Ch...

BARNEY KESSEL's signature (above) was removed from the pickguard of later versions when the guitarist switched his endorsement to the Gibson company.

SIDNEY M. KATZ (left) worked for Harmony in the early 1950s, but in 1955 together with a group of investors he bought Kay from founder Henry Kay Kuhrmeyer. Katz became president of the Kay Musical Instrument Co., and after enormous growth in the company's business he sold out in the 1960s to Seeburg, a manufacturer of jukeboxes also based in Chicago.

THE MARKETING of guitars became more focused as the 1950s progressed. While mail-order catalog companies reached the general buyer, the newly diverse musical interest groups were targeted by individual makers, such as Harmony with this 1957 ad (right) that was aimed at country players.

MAIL-ORDER GUITARS

The familiar name was 'the wish book', but formally it was called the *Sears, Roebuck and Company Catalog.* Until its demise in the 1980s it was one of the greatest documents of the pragmatic side of Western civilization, for in it one could find all the essential – and non-essential – artifacts of capitalist mass consumer culture. Everything one could

desire, from underclothes to living room furniture to guitars, graced its excess of a thousand pages, all available through the mail. And, beginning in the early 1950s, it was the Sears catalog (and many competitors) that made the dream of electric guitars a reality in homes across America.

The catalog phenomenon dates back to the end of the 19th century, when hordes of Europeans were flooding into the vast hinterland of America, farming the prairie and establishing towns. By the 1890s, farmers were selling crops for cash and buying goods from local general stores, which increasingly gained a reputation for selling at inflated prices, against which farmers staged protests.

Some retailers, including Richard Sears, saw an opportunity in this discontent. Sears' Minnesota watch shop relocated into the exploding manufacturing might of Chicago, with its far-reaching transportation network. Taking advantage of rural free delivery and parcel post, Sears and others determined to cut out

THE STRATOTONE's features (right) include stacked knobs and a 'Harmometal' body rim.

KAY's impressive chrome and plastic pickups (left) are often referred to as 'Kleenex Box' types thanks to their general shape and central oval 'slot'.

△ KAY BARNEY KESSEL ARTIST
Produced 1957-1960; this example c1958

Poll-winning jazzman Kessel endorsed a line of three Kay models that strikingly exemplified 1950s design and style.

1958

SEARS' 1959 catalog shows six electrics (left to right): Danelectro-made 'solid center body'; Kay-made Les Paul-like hollow-body; Danelectro-made bass; Kay-made hollow-body; and Harmony-made 'thinline'.

Kay Musical Instrument Company. Harmony was begun in 1892, and in 1916 was actually purchased by Sears to provide its stringed instruments. Harmony was sold to a group of its own executives in 1940, but continued to be Sears' largest and principal source. Danelectro was started in 1946 by Nathan Daniel, the man who designed Epiphone's Electar amplifiers of the late 1930s. From 1954 Danelectro was one of the largest manufacturers of Sears' catalog electric guitars.

Some of the brandnames that appeared on these catalog guitars of the 1950s included: Silvertone, for Sears (earlier Sears guitars had been called Supertone); Sherwood and Airline, for Montgomery Ward; Penncrest, for Penney's; Old Kraftsman, for Spiegel; and 'A', for Alden's. The brandname belonged to the retailer, and could be applied to guitars from different suppliers.

The catalog guitars were value-priced but that does not necessarily mean they were poor instruments. At the top end, many of these guitars were actually quite good, although often catalog guitars were not quite up to the same quality as the equivalent brandname instrument. For example, when Sears began to sell the Kay Thin Twin (see page 22/23) its Silvertone version had cheaper and hence thicker necks as well as just slightly less fancy cuts of wood than the Kay-branded guitar. At the bottom end the guitars were more humble, but still with some quality – remember, they could be returned if customers were not satisfied.

Working in tandem with the guitar mass manufacturers, the mass merchandisers followed market tastes like a shadow. As the 1950s began the styles of music in which electric guitars were most visible included Hawaiian, which had had a remarkable run of popularity for nearly half a century, and country & Western. Hawaiian music demanded little lap steels, which in some ways can be said to have fathered the electric guitar itself, while the country & Western bands were picking pedal steels and 'electrified' archtops, still top dogs of the guitar world. In response, early 1950s catalogs offered mainly Hawaiian lap steels and a few full-bodied, non-cutaway archtops with one or sometimes two pickups.

When in 1952 Kay introduced the cutaway electric to its archtop line, the catalogs very quickly incorporated it into their offerings. In around 1954 another Kay innovation, the Thin Twin, began to show up in the catalogs as well. Size-wise, the Thin Twin was somewhere between Gibson's ES-175 hollow-body and the new Les Paul. While it was hollow, it did have wood down the middle to reduce the feedback of its pickups. The Thin Twin was sold through the Sears, Montgomery Ward and Spiegel catalogs, carrying their house brandnames.

The solidbody electric guitar started on a slow curve in the early 1950s, eventually taking off mid-decade with the success of rock'n'roll. The first 'Spanish' solidbody electrics appeared in the Sears catalog in the spring of 1954, the Silvertone version of the Harmony Stratotone, a sort of mini-Les Paul with one or two pickups. These were offered only briefly, and by the fall 1954 catalog, Sears had switched to single-cutaway Danelectros, the presence of which increased as the decade progressed.

GIBSON's tag (above) noted the Les Paul's "long sustain", which would endear it to later generations of guitarists.

WHEN A GUITAR is as highly prized as the Les Paul Sunburst, even the tags (right) originally attached to the guitar become collectible. The orange label promotes Gibson's Sonomatic strings; the brown booklet offers care tips.

NEW! "DUAL PICKUP" ELECTRIC

$89⁹⁸

OUR FINEST!

$9 Down
$8 Monthly

- Thin body . . easier to hold, easier to play.
- Twin Electronic Pickups produce pure tone.
- 3-way Selector for bass, treble, or conventional.
- Twin volume and tone control knobs.

A beautiful hand-rubbed body . . . so thin, it's easy to hold. Yet this streamlined beauty has this advantage: It's wide enough to hold and play like a conventional guitar! Select curly maple top and back. Mahogany sides. 40⅝x14⅞ in. wide. *Amplifier not included.*
57 H 1381—Shpg. wt. 13 lbs. *$8 mo.*, *$8 mo.* . . . Cash $89.98
57 H 1382—Above with case. Shpg. wt. 16 lbs. Cash 99.98

$39⁹⁹ cash

$4 Down
$5 Monthly

Low Price!

"Hi-Low" Selector

Tone and volume control

SOLID BODY

NOW an *Electric* Spanish Guitar . . yours for only $39.99! Full professional 25¾-in. scale, yet only 36 in. long, 10½ in. wide. High-fidelity pickup unit. "Hi-Low" treble-bass selector switch. White enamel finish. *Amplifier not included. $4 down, $5 monthly.* Shpg. wt. 9 lbs.
57 H 1361 . . . . Cash $39.99
57 H 1362—Above with case. Wt. 10 lbs. *$4.50 down*. . . . 44.50
57 H 1363—Guitar with 2 pickups, 2 tone, 2 volume controls, 3-pos. selector switch. Shpg. wt. 9 lbs. *$6 down*. . . . Cash 59.98
57 H 1364—With case. Wt. 10 lbs. *$6.50 dn*. . . . Cash $64.50

Order amplifiers separately below at right

Stand $9.69

$32.50
Cash
Guitar only
$3.50 Down

$42.50
Cash
$4.50 Down
$5 Monthly

ELECTRIC HAWAIIAN GUITARS

D Good Quality. Sturdy hardwood body, shaded ivory and walnut color lacquer finish. Built-in magnetic pickup. Separate tone, volume controls. Brass-geared tuning pegs. Size 31½x9 in. Amplifier required. With 8-ft. cord, picks, and steel. *Home Study Book.* Shipping weights guitar 7 lbs.; with amplifier (L) at right 23 lbs. Order case 57H01486 on preceding page.
57 H 01319—Guitar Only. *$3.50 down* Cash $32.50
57 H 1329L—With amplifier (L) at right. *$7 Down $6 Month*. . . . . Cash $69.95

E Our Best. Streamlined design. Seasoned hardwood body. Black finish; white celluloid trim on top and edges. White plastic fingerboard. Magnetic pickup. Separate tone, volume controls. Nickel-plated hand rest. Brass-geared tuning pegs. 31½x9 in. Amplifier required. With 8-ft. cord, picks and steel. *Home Study Book.* Shpg. wts. guitar 9 lbs.; with amplifier (57H01542L) 34 lbs. Order case 57 H 01486.
57 H 01315—Guitar only . . . . Cash $42.50
57 H 1326L—With amplifier (K) at right *$10.50 Down, $9 Month*. . . . . . .Cash $104.95
57 H 3415—Hawaiian Electric Guitar Stand. [see

Guitar Strap $3.69

GOOD $44.95 Cash A
Guitar only $4.50 Down

BETTER $64.95 Cash B
$6.50 Down $6 Monthly

BEST $99.95 Cash C
$10.00 Down $8 Monthly

SILVERTONE ARCHED ELECTRIC SPANISH GUITARS

All with built-in high fidelity pickup; Tone, volume Controls, Study Book

WANT TO BE MORE POPULAR? Play an electric guitar. Sound just like those played on radio and TV.

Choose your SILVERTONE from our large selection. Each one built for lasting service, beautiful design.

A Good Quality. Firmly bonded joints won't pull apart. Spruce top, maple back and sides. Top and back edges bound with white celluloid. Durable Brazilian rosewood fingerboard. Adjustable built-in pickup. Separate tone, volume control knobs. 40 x 15¼ in. Shpg. wts. guitars 11 lbs. With amplifiers 26 lbs.
57 H 01322L—Blonde finish guitar *$4.50 Dn.*, *$5 Mo.* Cash $44.95
57 H 1139L—Above with amplifier (L) below. *$8 Dn.* Cash $79.95
57 H 01320L—Brown finish, shaded sunburst. *$4.50 Dn*.Cash $44.95
57 H 1380L—Above with amplifier (L) below. *$8 Dn.* Cash $79.95

Bobby Lee's No-Mishap Guitar Strap. For true, balanced position.
57 H 3604—Shpg. wt. 4 oz. . .$3.69

B Better Quality model has select spruce top; curly maple back and sides . . . all firmly bonded together for extra durability. Entire finish carefully hand-polished to a glowing luster. Celluloid trim on top, bottom edges, and fingerboard protects your instrument from scratches. Built-in pickup is adjustable. Separate tone, volume control knobs. 41x16¼ in. Shipping weights guitars 12 lbs.; with amplifiers 34 lbs.
57 H 01373L—Blonde finish Guitar. *$6.50 Dn.*, *$6 Mo*. . . .Cash $64.95
57 H 1383L—Above with amplifier (K) below. *$12.50 Down, $10 Mouth.* Cash. $124.95
57 H 01371—Brown with shaded sunburst. *$6.50 Dn.*, Cash $64.95
57 H 1327L—Above with amplifier (K) below. *$12.50 Down, $10 Mouth.*, Cash $124.95

C Our Best Quality Electric Arched Guitar. Ever-popular cutaway design lets you play high notes with complete freedom. Hand-selected matched spruce top; choice maple back, sides. Beautifully hand-polished. Individual enclosed patent heads; six mother-of-pearl position markers. Sturdy 5-ply neck. Tone, volume controls. 10-ft. cord, pick. *Home Study Book* included. 42x17 in. Shpg. wts. guitar 12 lbs.; guitar with amplifier 41 lbs. *Order Case 57H0727 L.* or *57H728F on preceding page.*
57 H 01354L—Blonde finish. $99.95
57 H 1374L—With Amplifier (J) below. *$18 dn.*. . . Cash $179.95
57H01356L—Mahog.finish.Cash 99.95
57 H 1376L [

It's Eas[
Dual-Unli[
or a [

BIG SEL[

H Our Be[ful am[
Two gia[tifier. B[trol foot[tensity [for eac[pilot li[leathe[17x9½[A.C. [
57 H [

Our [but [tube[plu[One [pla[For [list[or[
57 [
M[

SHOP THE EASY MODERN WAY
by TELEPHONE
For number to call see pages 5–7

SEARS, ROEBUCK's 1954 catalog (left, with cover shown below left) displays its Silvertone brand version of the Kay Thin Twin (top left) alongside Harmony- and Kay-made hollow-body electrics.

Sears' first solidbody electric, its version of the Harmony Stratotone, is shown center left. Below this are a couple of Harmony-made Hawaiian electric guitars as well as a Silvertone amplifier.

THE MOST CELEBRATED Les Paul Sunbursts, or 'bursts' (right), are those whose bodies exhibit the most outrageous wood patterns ('figure' or 'flame'). Figure is a random fluke in wood: some Les Paul Sunbursts are highly attractive, others extremely plain.

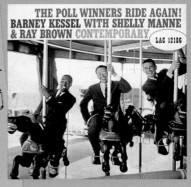
the middlemen who drove prices so high, and began to sell directly to customers at home through catalogs. The first Sears catalog with a full line of consumer goods, including guitars, was produced in 1896.

The idea was phenomenally successful. 'Shop at Sears and save' was more than a sales slogan, it was the truth. It would eventually make Sears the world's largest retailer.

By the 1950s, mail-order catalogs had become a major part of the retailing landscape and were ideally suited to serve the expanding nation. The Depression and World War were over, and times were relatively good. The Baby Boom was in high gear. Pent-up consumer demand, after years of deprivation, was enormous. While most cities, large and small, had department stores, populations were moving out into suburban developments. Shopping malls had not yet been invented. People turned to their wish books. During the 1950s, the huge Sears, Roebuck and Company catalog was by far the most influential, but there were many other catalog retailers, including Montgomery Ward, J.C. Penney, Spiegel, and Alden's. All sold guitars during the 1950s.

From the early days on, the catalog merchants sold what would be considered student, or beginner, up to intermediate grade instruments. The premise behind mass merchandise catalogs was value-for-the-dollar, and thus they did not try to sell more expensive, better brandname guitars such as Gibson or Martin – although Gibson, at least, provided some budget instruments to the catalogs.

In a way, the story of catalog guitars closely parallels that of the large American mass manufacturers of guitars of the time, all of whom thrived on supplying the catalog business. The primary suppliers during the 1950s were the Chicago powerhouses, Kay and Harmony, and later the New Jersey-based Danelectro company.

Kay dated back to 1890, first as the Groehsl company, then as Stromberg-Voisinet and finally in the 1930s as the

△ HARMONY STRATOTONE NEWPORT H42/1
Produced 1957-1959; this example 1957

Typical of the many budget-priced solidbody guitars made to cash in on Fender's success, the Newport was at $80 a cheap product of the Chicago-based Harmony operation.

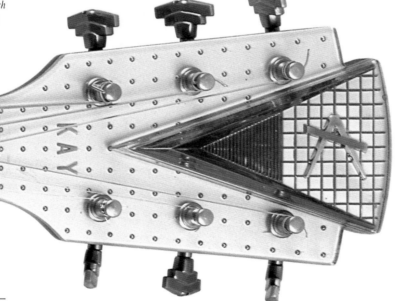

▽ KAY BARNEY KESSEL PRO
Produced 1957-1960; this example c1958

The Kessel Pro, at $200, was one of three Kessel models at the top of Kay's pricelist. The Artist sold for $300, while the Jazz Special at $400 was Kay's most expensive guitar.

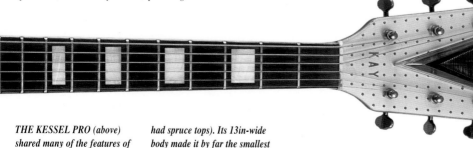

THE KESSEL PRO (above) shared many of the features of the other two Kay Kessels, but was of semi-solid construction with a maple top (the hollow-body Artist and Jazz Special had spruce tops). Its 13in-wide body made it by far the smallest of the trio, and it was generally intended to compete with guitars such as Gibson's various Les Paul models.

INJECTION molded plastics made a big impact on 1950s design, seldom with more effect than this spectacular headstock (above and left), often called the 'Kelvinator' head by collectors because of its similarity to the refrigerator company's logo. Kay emphasized the unusually upscale nature of the Kessel line of models by using a gold theme in their promotion (as in the 1958 ad shown, right). While the Kessels enhanced Kay's image, they did not last long.

Framus

"Billy Lorento"
Model

Scale 24⅛". Length 42". Body 20¾" x 17¼" x 2⅛".
New in construction, shape, tone variation and tone combination. Fitted with two mikes, one at the end of neck for softness; the other, nearby bridge, for intensiveness and brilliance. This revolutionary innovation leads to unheard-of facilitation for a soloist in playing the instrument.

Cash Price £66 . 10 . 10
Deposit £6 . 0 . 0 and 12 monthly payments of £5 . 11 . 0
or 18 monthly payments of £3 . 17 . 4 or 24 monthly payments of £2 . 12 . 3
Special Case for this model £10 . 16 . 0

BELL MUSIC was the leading mail-order supplier of guitars in the UK in the 1950s, with a catalog (left) that introduced guitars to many fledgling stars. Bell's various imported lines included Framus guitars of Germany, with one model (far left) designed by guitarist Billy Lorento, better known later as pickup designer Bill Lawrence.

Toward the end of the 1950s Hawaiian lap steels dwindled to a single offering, and where once non-cutaway electric archtops dominated, cutaways now ruled. By around 1958 or so, in response to the growing folk boom, the catalogs were offering flat-tops with pickups mounted in the soundholes. By 1959, Danelectros were getting space pressure from other hollowbody Les Paul-shaped guitars, including versions of Kay's Thinline series and Harmony's Jupiter. Finally, 1959 saw the introduction of the first thin-body electric, a three-pickup Harmony.

It's impossible to underestimate the impact catalog guitars had on the development of popular music because they were often the first guitars of many future stars. Those who got their start on a guitar from a catalog include players as diverse as Duane Allman of the Allman Brothers, Elvis Presley's guitarist Scotty Moore, slide king Ry Cooder, Cliff Gallup of Gene Vincent's band, and bluesmen Muddy Waters and Freddie King, among a host of others.

The 1950s were just a prelude to the guitar-drenched 1960s, as the cresting post-war Baby Boom swept into high adolescence. But it was the 1950s which created the desire for electric guitars, and the 'wish books' that brought those dreams home. ■ MICHAEL WRIGHT

A GREAT YEAR for guitar-fueled records: Duane Eddy's 'Rebel Rouser', Eddie Cochran's 'Summertime Blues', Link Wray's 'The Rumble'... and Chuck Berry's 'Johnny B Goode' plays his guitar like ringing a bell.

JAPAN and India change to the metric system; America launches a moon rocket that misses; blues popularizer W.C. Handy dies; the artist to be known as Prince is born.

PRIVATE EYE Peter Gunn begins his TV investigations amid a moody jazz soundtrack.

THE CAMPAIGN for Nuclear Disarmament (CND) is started in the UK, with its first protest march from London to the Atomic Weapons Research Establishment at Aldermaston. Over 9000 scientists from 44 countries petition the UN to end nuclear weapons tests.

RECORDING companies decide to adopt the Westrex 45/45 stereo system, and some of the big labels release the first stereo records in the summer.

THESE 'CROWN' inlays (below) had first appeared on Gibson's revised ES-150 model in 1950.

TV OWNERSHIP in the US is rocketing, with sets in over 75 per cent of homes. And TV makers like Philco encourage viewers to move the TV around the house, advertising new portable models such as the Slender Seventeen (left).

△ GIBSON LES PAUL 'SUNBURST'
Produced 1958-1960; this example 1959

While mail-order catalogs churned out budget-price guitars, makers of more upscale instruments reassessed their lines. Gibson's gold-top Les Paul model had dipped in popularity, so in 1958 Gibson tried to regenerate interest by giving it the company's more traditional cherry sunburst finish. Production did increase modestly during 1959 and 1960, but the Sunburst model was dropped during 1960 after fewer than 2000 had been made. Years later, this 1958-1960 Sunburst has become the most valuable vintage guitar, with prime 'flamed' examples regularly fetching high five-figure sums today and often consigned to bank vaults.

GIBSON managed to exploit the name of its most famous endorsee in many ways, as demonstrated by this retailer's counter display for picks, allegedly "personally selected and tested by Les Paul".

THE SUNBURST has Kluson Deluxe tuners with 'tulip' plastic buttons (above) that tend to deteriorate with age.

ITALIAN LEATHER LOOK   FLAME   ALLIGATOR TAN   ALLIGATOR V

Most slender of all... even the back is beautiful!

BLUES GUITARS *by Paul Trynka*

As the 1950s unfolded, the old generation of acoustic blues players gave way to a new wave of players who were electric in every sense. In just a few years musicians such as Big Bill Broonzy or Memphis Minnie became outmoded, and in their place came a brash, extrovert troupe – Muddy Waters, Guitar Slim, Howlin' Wolf – with the sound and image of the electric guitar at the heart of their appeal. They would change the sound of popular music forever.

DESPITE CHESS's failure to sign the hugely commercial Jimmy Reed, Chess ruled as Chicago's premier blues label in the 1950s, releasing influential and commercially successful recordings by Muddy Waters (above), Howlin' Wolf, Little Walter, Sonny Boy Williamson II and many more. The label made full use of Chicago's overflowing pool of talent, and the city's guitarists became accustomed to midnight calls from the Chess studios asking if they could perform a particularly tricky part. Although Muddy Waters and Howlin' Wolf both ran legendarily tight outfits, in the studio they would regularly call on the likes of Freddie King or Buddy Guy to augment their usual band.

BLUES GUITARS

In many respects the electric blues scene of 1950s Chicago was born in the more rural surroundings of Helena, Arkansas, where Robert Lockwood Jr, adopted son of Robert Johnson, could be heard playing the electric guitar alongside Sonny Boy Williamson every week on the influential King Biscuit Time radio show, from 1941. Lockwood single-handedly converted seemingly all of Mississippi's guitarists to the electric instrument, and it would be these players – Muddy Waters, Jimmy Rogers, Elmore James – who would in fact go on to form the backbone of the emerging Chicago scene.

Over the same period T-Bone Walker evangelized for the electric guitar over on the West Coast, with the result that by 1947 or 1948 practically every young blues musician was converted to the sound of the new instrument. The electric guitar was hip, it was loud, it was better for single-string lead work… and if you were working on the street it helped you earn more tips. That was the reason that Jimmy Rogers fitted a DeArmond pickup to his Sears acoustic, and when he took his Mississippi bandmate Muddy Waters down to the Chicago Musical Instruments store to get a pickup for his own guitar, a musical revolution was born. Waters' first electric hit, 'I Can't Be Satisfied', dates from 1948, the same year that John Lee Hooker cut 'Boogie Chillen'. These two flagbearers for a new electric era were joined by musicians such as Gatemouth Brown in 1949, B.B. King in 1951, Howlin' Wolf in 1952 and Guitar Slim in 1953, and with the huge explosion of new talent, guitar playing developed at a dizzying pace.

Looking back at evocative old black-and-white photos of blues performers of the late 1940s and into the 1950s, it's hard to believe that many of them were at the cutting edge of technology. But that was exactly the case. From the moment the Fender Telecaster first rolled out of Fullerton, California, it appeared in the hands of blues players: for example, a 1950 photo of Clarence Gatemouth Brown and his brother James 'Widemouth' Brown shows them both sporting Telecasters – Clarence's a black model with studded decoration that could even be one of the two-pickup Esquires which preceded the Tele. At a time when the industry derided the new-fangled Telecaster as a toilet seat with strings attached, blues guitarists embraced it. The

GIBSON's double-cut Junior was the company's first with its new cherry finish.

58

GIBSON's Les Paul guitar, overlooked in some musical quarters, was a favorite of many Chicago blues guitarists, including Muddy Waters (right). Others who played a Les Paul in the 1950s included Hubert Sumlin and Jody Williams from Howlin' Wolf's band, Freddie King, and Buddy Guy, who went on to popularize the Strat after his Gibson was stolen from a club.

same would be true of other pioneering guitars throughout the 1950s, as blues musicians were at the forefront of those exploring the sounds of solidbody instruments, semi-solid guitars such as the Gibson ES-335, and the sonic possibilities of over-driven amplifiers.

Blues of the 1950s boasts many musical mavericks, but it's fair to say that the music can generally be divided into three distinct schools. First comes Chicago blues, as epitomized by Muddy Waters or Elmore James – in its early form, essentially the Mississippi blues of Robert Johnson but cranked up and electrified. Then there was the B.B. King or Lowell Fulson school of blues: increasingly sophisticated, with more gospel influence and single-string guitar soloing, largely derived from T-Bone Walker and Louis Jordan. Thirdly, Texas blues was best exemplified by

HOWLIN' WOLF (above) learned guitar from Delta blues pioneer Charley Patton in the 1920s. Wolf later formed one of the South's first electric blues bands when he teamed up with Willie Johnson, who'd adopted an electric guitar after seeing Sonny Boy Williamson. Wolf's genius for spotting talent was confirmed by his subsequent recruitment of the mercurial Hubert Sumlin, who would craft memorable guitar riffs on classic Wolf tracks such as 'Wang Dang Doodle' and 'Killing Floor'.

▽ GIBSON LES PAUL TV

Produced 1955-1959; this example 1958

The TV model was a light-colored version of the Les Paul Junior. The name may have been an attempt to gain from Les Paul's mid-1950s TV outing, 'The Les Paul & Mary Ford Show'.

THE JUNIOR and TV were the simplest solidbody models in the Gibson line of the time, with basic hardware, single pickup and plain decoration.

△ GIBSON LES PAUL JUNIOR

Produced 1954-1961; this example 1960

Nineteen fifty-eight was Gibson's year of the double-cutaway. The company reacted to the requests of players who wanted more room at the top of the neck to reach the higher frets for lead playing. Not only did Gibson introduce the entirely new double-cut ES-335 and 345 semi-hollow models during 1958 (see p69) but also in that year the company radically modified the shape of the solidbody Les Paul Junior and TV models to the new style shown here. The Junior's fresh look was also enhanced with a new cherry red finish. The design lasted until 1961, when the Les Paul models would be produced with the 'SG' shape.

TV, JUNIOR and Special had started life with a single-cutaway body (still on view in this 1957 catalog, left). During 1958 and '59 a revised double-cutaway style (as seen above) was introduced.

EPIPHONE

Epiphone Inc. · 210 Bush Street · Kalamazoo, Michigan

guitars
basses
amplifiers

EPIPHONE was bought by Gibson in May 1957, and while Gibson had expected only to get Epiphone's upright bass business, it actually ended up with virtually the entire company: guitars, basses, amps and more (as reflected on the Gibson-Epiphone catalog shown, left). Production of Gibson's revised line of Epiphone models was underway by 1958.

THE STANDARD tailpiece on Epiphone hollow-body guitars was the company's unusual 'Frequensator' unit (see p8), but along with makers such as Gibson and Gretsch, Epiphone also offered the Bigsby vibrato tailpiece (below) as an option.

Gatemouth Brown: open-E tunings, the use of the capo, and picking with the fingers were all typical Texas techniques used by the likes of Brown, Johnny Guitar Watson, and Guitar Slim. As the 1950s progressed, these different growths cross-pollinated.

When electric blues first hit Chicago the music essentially derived from 1930s blues. Both Muddy Waters and John Lee Hooker (based in Detroit but hugely popular in Chicago) offered updated versions of down-home Mississippi blues. Their music was therefore completely appropriate for a northern, urban, African-American audience which had only recently moved from the rural South. In some respects, if you ignore the electric guitars, the music seemed something of a throwback compared to the sophisticated urban music purveyed by Lonnie Johnson, Big Bill Broonzy or even Louis Jordan.

'NEW YORK' pickups (below; the name refers to Epiphone's original home) continued to be used until around 1961.

EPIPHONE's eccentric early multi-button pickup switching system was replaced with these conventional controls (above).

△ EPIPHONE EMPEROR
Produced 1958-1969; this example c1959

'Emperor' was a model name from Epiphone's pre-Gibson years when production was based in New York (see p8), but under the new owners this Kalamazoo-made version received a more conventional control layout. Other hollow-body electrics in the new Epi line included the Sheraton, Broadway and Century.

electric guitar, which would reach a new plateau as a lead instrument over the same period.

B.B. King exemplifies the progression in electric guitar styles throughout the 1950s. Starting out as a strictly Delta player, influenced by his cousin Bukka White, King absorbed the jazzy soloing of Lonnie Johnson, the single-note lead technique of T-Bone Walker, and the laid-back jump blues-influenced sound of Lowell Fulson. His work with Robert Lockwood, a fan of jazz saxophone as well as a great Robert Johnson exponent, must also have exerted a profound influence. King's first recordings for the Bullet and RPM labels were spiky-sounding affairs, many of them boasting the distinct solidbody tones of a Fender Esquire or Stratocaster.

However, when Gibson's ES-335 debuted in 1958, King immediately purchased the radical and often under-rated semi-solid instrument. Asked why, King concisely runs through every one of the 335's sales points: light weight, combination of solid and acoustic tone, thin body, and good upper-fret access. Just as the ES-335 brought the

But as the decade progressed, Chicago blues became more diverse and sophisticated, as perhaps best exemplified by Waters' harp player, Little Walter.

Walter was really the first player to explore the possibilities of the amplified harmonica, which he termed the 'Mississippi saxophone'. Amplified, the harp sounded fatter, jazzier, and more suited for solo or lead work, and when Walter teamed up with the musically-educated Myers brothers in 1952, he helped change the musical emphasis from the rhythmic Delta slide sound to a more open, melodically-led form of music. Exactly the same progression would take place in the sound of the

ONCE GIBSON had taken over, the revitalized Epiphone announced a fresh line of hollow-body electric guitars (stylized with an upright bass on this 1958 brochure, below). Five models kicked off the hollow electrics in 1958. One,

the deep-body $310 Broadway, was continued from the existing line, while another four were new or revised thinline types: the $145 Century, $245 Zephyr, $410 Sheraton, and the top-of-the-line $660 Emperor.

the unequalled tone of EPIPHONE

...in exciting new GUITARS AMPLIFIERS BASSES

World-famous quality since 1873

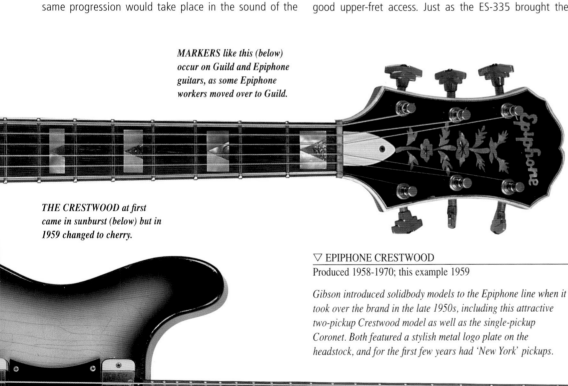

▽ EPIPHONE CRESTWOOD
Produced 1958-1970; this example 1959

Gibson introduced solidbody models to the Epiphone line when it took over the brand in the late 1950s, including this attractive two-pickup Crestwood model as well as the single-pickup Coronet. Both featured a stylish metal logo plate on the headstock, and for the first few years had 'New York' pickups.

MICKEY BAKER (left) came to fame through the 1957 US hit, 'Love Is Strange', which he recorded with vocalist Sylvia Vanderpool, as Mickey & Sylvia. But Baker's net was spread wider than pop hits: he played as a session guitarist backing artists from Little Willie John to Big Joe Turner, and made his own records like this 1959 Atlantic LP (left).

THE JAZZMASTER that Mickey Baker is playing (right) is an early anodized pickguard version – and it looks as if Baker has tried to protect the fragile surface of this material from his strumming with a piece of card stuck between the pickups.

hollow-body jazz guitar up to date, King brought blues lead guitar up to date, perfecting a fluid, almost vocal guitar style which would influence countless numbers of blues players including guitarists such as Buddy Guy, Otis Rush, and Freddie and Albert King.

In the early 1950s King's fame as a guitar hero was far exceeded by a much brasher and more extrovert character who would change the sound of blues and R&B guitar in an equally profound way. Modern guitar history often states that it was the likes of The Kinks or Eric Clapton who introduced distortion and overdrive techniques into the guitarist's armory, but Guitar Slim's huge 1953 crossover

FENDER JAZZMASTER
Produced 1958-1980, re-issued 1986; this example 1959

The Jazzmaster was launched in 1958 as Fender's top solidbody, at $329 some $50 more expensive than the Strat. At that sort of price Fender could not resist tagging its new Jazzmaster as "America's finest electric guitar... unequaled in performance and design features". Immediately striking was the unusual offset-waist body shape and, for the first time on a Fender, a rosewood fingerboard. The 'lock-off' vibrato system was new, too, aimed at preventing tuning problems if a string should break, and the Jazzmaster had an elaborate new control layout.

EARLY EXAMPLES of the Jazzmaster came with an anodized aluminum pickguard,

but this was soon replaced with a plastic unit in white or tortoiseshell (above).

CONTROLS on the Jazzmaster (left) were intricate. A small slide-switch above the front pickup selected between two individual circuits, intended to allow the player to preset a rhythm sound and a lead sound, and then switch at will between the two. This dual-circuit idea was adapted from a layout that Fender's production manager Forrest White had designed back in the 1940s when he built guitars as a hobby. The sound of the new Jazzmaster was richer and warmer than players were used to from Fender, and the guitar had what many felt were 'un-Fender' looks. The fact that the Jazzmaster was so different when compared with other Fenders may explain its relative lack of success.

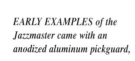

CLARENCE 'Gatemouth' Brown has a Gibson L-5 here (about 1949, left) but soon switched to a Telecaster. His use of Fender's new guitar would influence Albert Collins and Guitar Slim to play a Tele.

GUITAR SLIM's outrageous stagecraft, characteristic guitar sounds and gospel-influenced songwriting anticipated much of rock'n'roll, soul and R&B, even the work of Jimi Hendrix. Although not the first player to put a distorted electric guitar on record, Slim was the first to use distortion as an integral part of his style. He also stood out from other players thanks to his distinctive personal style: he would flaunt red suits, green shoes, hair dyed any color from silver to blue, 120-feet guitar cords, and a guitar strap made from fishing line. When Gibson launched the Les Paul guitar Slim bought one instantly (he is seen with a gold-top in the photo, left), but he's also known to have played Fender Strats and Teles.

hit 'The Things I Used To Do' boasted a distinctive, heavily distorted guitar sound. The influence of innovators such as Guitar Slim and B.B. King meant that by the end of the 1950s Chicago blues became more and more technically sophisticated. The Chess company, particularly their in-house songwriter Willie Dixon, pioneered many influential techniques. Dixon in particular was intent that each prospective single should boast a catchy title and vocal hook, a distinctive guitar riff, and an individual rhythm, and he experimented with different guitarists for a particular feel. In the competitive Chicago circuit new techniques spread like wildfire, aided by the Chicago Musical Instruments retail store on 18th and Halsted which reportedly would lend instruments to influential players in prototype 'endorsement' deals. Their tactics worked: lending a Fender Precision to Little Walter and Muddy Waters' bassist Dave Myers helped establish the electric bass in the city, while the store's regular customer, Earl Hooker, was almost without fail the very first on the block with the newest, latest and shiniest instrument. As Otis Rush recalls, "Earl Hooker always used to be coming by with all kinds of gimmicks. All the musicians I knew didn't

have any stuff, but Earl was always coming by with new guitars, he had a guitar with two necks, and he sorta turned me on to the Strat."

According to Buddy Guy, Earl Hooker was the first player to realize that the Fender Bassman amplifier, on which the later Marshall units would be based, gave a fatter and more overdriven sound than the company's other guitar combos. Take into account the fact that by the later 1950s many of the city's guitarists were exploiting the inherently fat sound of Gibson humbuckers or the typically cutting sounds of the Strat's 'in-between' pickup-switching options, and it becomes obvious that in many ways the development of blues guitar playing throughout the 1950s anticipated that of white rock in the 1960s. It's no coincidence that the commercial but powerful sound of late-1950s guitarists such as Howlin' Wolf or Muddy Waters, based on distinctive rhythms and catchy, over-amplified guitar riffs, would effectively become a primer for late-1960s Led Zeppelin. Sadly, by the time that Chicago blues were taken up by the so-called British Invasion of the early 1960s, the music would be regarded as outmoded in its heartland. ■ PAUL TRYNKA

FENDER introduced a new, enlarged headstock design (above) for the Jazzmaster from its inception. This same larger shape would be adopted by the Fender company for use on the Stratocaster model during the mid-1960s.

WITH THE JAZZMASTER as its most expensive model in 1958, Fender emphasized in ads of the time (left) that the company was able to appeal to a wide range of players with its full line of guitars, from the cheapest 'student' models such as the $119.50 Musicmaster or $149.50 Duo-Sonic up to the 'professional' Jazzmaster at $329.50. As a comparison, Gibson's electric solidbody line at the time went from the $120 Les Paul Junior to the $375 Les Paul Custom.

COLLECTABILITY *by Stan Jay & Larry Wexer*

In today's 'vintage' guitar market, certain electric guitars from the 1950s are more sought after than instruments from any other period. Collectors demand total originality and pristine condition of the prized 1950s classics, while players wonder how a small production run or a particular paint job can add huge amounts to a guitar's value and may consign it to the bank vault rather than the rehearsal room.

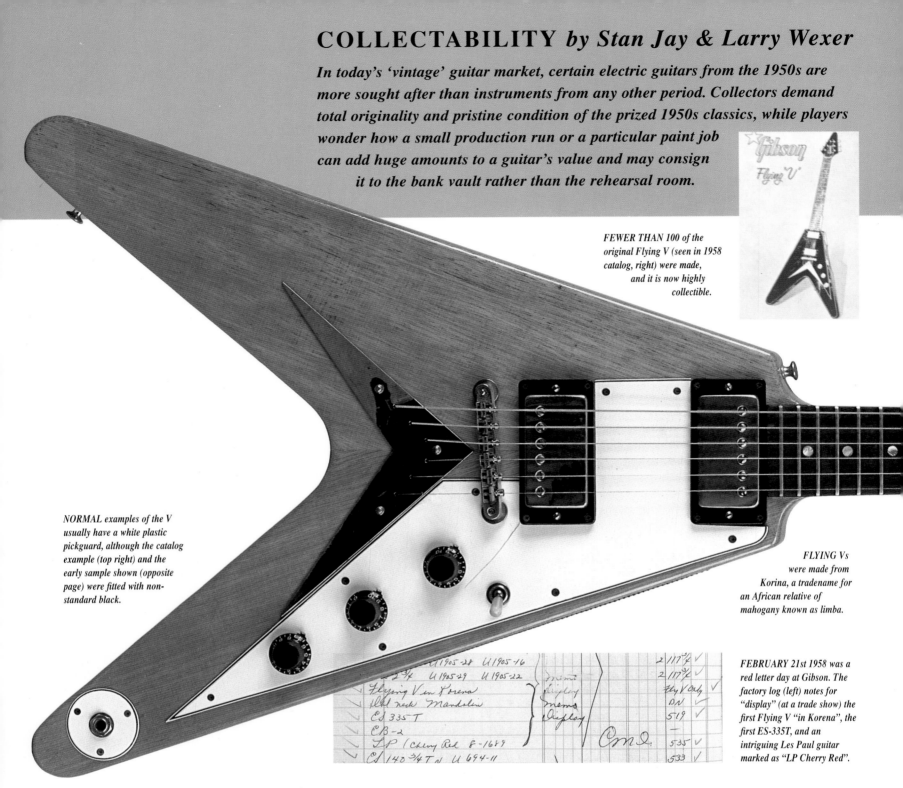

FEWER THAN 100 of the original Flying V (seen in 1958 catalog, right) were made, and it is now highly collectible.

NORMAL examples of the V usually have a white plastic pickguard, although the catalog example (top right) and the early sample shown (opposite page) were fitted with non-standard black.

FLYING Vs were made from Korina, a tradename for an African relative of mahogany known as limba.

FEBRUARY 21st 1958 was a red letter day at Gibson. The factory log (left) notes for "display" (at a trade show) the first Flying V "in Korena", the first ES-335T, and an intriguing Les Paul guitar marked as "LP Cherry Red".

COLLECTABILITY

The post-World War II era became an American cultural crucible in the 1950s. This was a time of economic prosperity, technological advancements, and the beginnings of social rebellion and introspection as a reaction to stifling conformism. Cultural icons of the period included larger-than-life personalities teeming with sexual energy, as well as objects which represent bold statements of the American aesthetic self-image.

The post-war era was characterized by many as a fresh start – a 'year one' – in which to begin anew and stumble headlong into the modern age. This feeling became an underlying current in 1950s culture. People sought to move ahead and to embrace new technologies. They perceived change as positive, and new things were considered an improvement over the old.

Many of the previous generations' household devices and fixtures were literally thrown away. The Tiffany style lamps which hung in the dining room were, unbelievably by today's sensibilities, relegated to the attic, or, more shatteringly, tossed without thought into the trash heap.

The automobile market is symptomatic of how the commercial marketplace behaved during the 1950s. Redesigned models came out every year or two, which helped engender the desire for the constantly newer, improved style. Some of these shapes were replete with sexual innuendo. As Americans felt more secure of their world position, the collective ego was expressed by these large two-ton luxury liners of the road. With each passing year cars had more gadgets, louder radios, bigger fins, more horsepower, and longer chassis. The aesthetics of the 1950s automobile and other modernistic designs – the vertical vacuum cleaner, abstract shaped coffee tables, lamps, and even Tupperware – saw a further expression in electric guitar designs of the period.

When we think of our idols, there is usually a guitar in hand (their hand, not ours; well, maybe ours). In wishing to emulate our heroes, we seek to own their original equipment. We see Elvis with his blond 1950s J-200 acoustic and Scotty Moore with his Super 400CES, and Chuck Berry with the ES-350T. The 1950s was the period when all of these Gibson models originated or flourished, and they came into being at the same time that the confluence of the major streams of American traditional musics came to form rock'n'roll.

Unlike previous decades, the 1950s saw successful American musicians using the latest equipment – part of the ethos of the 1950s was to be shown in pictures with shiny new stuff. When these new instruments became worn they were seen as 'used' replaceable guitars, not worthy of great reverence beyond their utility value.

Trends in popular music from the late 1950s onward resulted in individuals buying instruments that enabled them to create music of their own. In the 1940s you bought the records and listened to the radio. By the late 1950s you went out and got a guitar and a bass and soundproofed the garage. Manufacturers were pressured

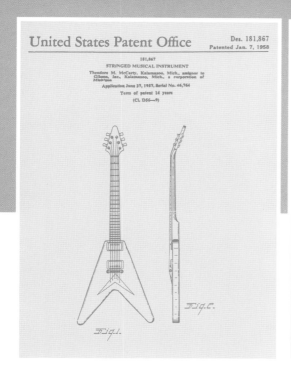

GIBSON decided that Fender's generally more flamboyant solidbody guitars were beating its traditional instruments in visual appeal, and launched two new 'Modernistic' models in 1958. The Flying V and the Explorer (see p66) abandoned conventional style, featuring original, boldly adventurous designs. But the guitars proved too radical: public response was negative, and very few were sold. Result: a prime 'vintage' rarity today, worth a fortune. A third Modernistic Gibson, the Moderne, was planned but never made it into production, even though a patent for the design was filed in summer 1957 (left, alongside Flying V patent).

△ GIBSON FLYING V

Produced 1958-1959, various re-issues; this example 1959

Publicized by Gibson as "an asset to the combo musician with a flair for showmanship", the Flying V failed in fact to excite any kind of musician, and sales were poor. Gibson shipped 81 of the $247.50 Flying V in 1958 and 17 in 1959, while an estimated 20 more were assembled in the early 1960s.

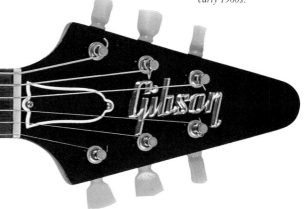

▽ GIBSON FLYING V

Produced 1958-1959, various re-issues; this example c1957

This is a pre-production Flying V sent by Gibson to its case supplier, Geib of Chicago, in 1957 so that a special fitted case could be designed for the unusual new instrument. In return for its industriousness, Geib was allowed to keep the guitar – a valuable gift, as it turned out.

THIS early V (above) has a gold logo; most models, like the one in the main picture, have a silver-colored version.

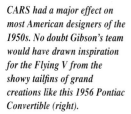

CARS had a major effect on most American designers of the 1950s. No doubt Gibson's team would have drawn inspiration for the Flying V from the showy tailfins of grand creations like this 1956 Pontiac Convertible (right).

America's Number 1 Road Car...

to build many times the numbers of instruments that they had leisurely made before. (Gibson, for example, made 317 natural and sunburst ES-335s in 1958, and in 1967 they built 5718 of them.) As the companies continued to make minor model changes, at a certain point these changes were no longer improvements. And as we reached the late 1960s musicians began to realize that the quality of contemporary instruments was in many cases no longer equal to the quality of those that had been made in the past. This, in conjunction with musicians trying to recapture the sounds of their heroes, caused players to look for the older guitars, and since then the 'vintage' market has come into being.

But why are some instruments considered 'vintage', and others just 'used'? Vintage guitars are made of materials, or with a degree of workmanship, not exhibited on current models. A vintage guitar is an original, having specific characteristics stemming from its time of manufacture. As much as major companies have, recently, tried to reproduce these originals, today's copies are very close, but are not exact replicas. The intangible qualities which are so evident to knowledgeable players and discerning collectors are what set the fine vintage instruments apart from their latter day counterparts.

The original electric guitars of the 1950s were made in limited quantities. Many models were newly introduced and met with only limited success. Manufacturers kept producing new ideas, some of which were accepted by the buying public, and some of which were not. A classic example is the Gibson Modernistic guitars. In trying to escape Gibson's stodgy image, Ted McCarty and his colleagues designed rocket-shaped guitars which didn't take off in the marketplace, including the Flying V, the Explorer and the mythical Moderne which is seen even more rarely than Howard Hughes hitchhiking on the highway. Less than 150 Modernistic guitars were produced in total, making this unsuccessful endeavor into what

GIBSON'S PATENT (below) of 1957 is for the design that became the Explorer. Most examples have a long, drooping headstock with the tuners in a line on one side, but some early models (like that in the main picture) have the V-shaped head of the patent. These early versions of the Explorer are sometimes referred to as Futura models.

United States Patent Office
Des. 181,865
Patented Jan. 7, 1958

181,865
STRINGED MUSICAL INSTRUMENT
Theodore M. McCarty, Kalamazoo, Mich., assignor to Gibson, Inc., Kalamazoo, Mich., a corporation of Michigan

Application June 20, 1957, Serial No. 46,674

Term of patent 14 years

(Cl. D56—9)

Fig.1.   Fig.2.

GIBSON's designers' main departure from conventional guitar design was to use straight lines for the Explorer (below) and the Flying V, rather than the rounded forms more generally employed.

THE SWITCH below the back pickup (left) is not original; it was added by previous owner Rick Derringer.

CONTROLS on the Explorer (right) and Flying V were different from Gibson's usual two-pickup layout: here, the player has a volume per pickup and an overall tone.

today are considered as incredibly rare and expensive guitars. Meanwhile, in Brooklyn, Gretsch guitars were made in car colors (green, orange, white, bamboo yellow, copper mist) with Cadillac tailpieces and western motifs (dead cows, cacti, cattle brands, and leather-tooled side-covers and cases). These kitsch accouterments are, oddly, typical of the 1950s.

Even the most modest and affordable old guitars, like those sold at the Sears, Roebuck store or through their mail-order catalog under the name Silvertone, had a primitive, wacky quality and unique tone which endear themselves to us, even now.

Pioneering dealers such as Harry West and Izzy Young in New York and Jon & Deirdre Lundberg and Marc Silber in California established between the late 1940s and the late 1960s the idea that old guitars were potentially better than

new ones and thus worth a premium. As time went on a few other individuals began to see buying and selling vintage American instruments as a viable source of income, and set up businesses whose purpose it was to find, restore, market and actually sell these fretted jewels of American craftsmanship to an eager and hungry audience. Today there are over 250 dealers advertising their inventories every month in magazines such as Vintage Guitar and 20th Century Guitar.

In folklore there has always been a feeling that the true lore is something that is rapidly disappearing. In vintage guitars, the same feeling has caused people to become collectors, and amass and hoard their favorite six-string babies, lest they become unobtainable. At the same time as this occurred with acoustic instruments in the late 1960s, one began to see a recording artist like Eric Clapton playing

a 1959 sunburst Les Paul through a 1960s Marshall amplifier.

Mike Bloomfield, playing with Paul Butterfield's Blues Band, was seen with black-guard, early 1950s Telecasters, then P-90 gold-top Les Pauls, and ultimately with a PAF-equipped 'burst. In this way visibly prominent artists defined the instruments which would be taken seriously by professionals, and this engendered vintage lust in musicians at large. Clapton still exerts a tremendous influence on the market, even today. His appearance on a TV show in the mid-1990s with an early-issue dot-neck ES-335 spurred a rash of phone calls to dealers and, in fact, resuscitated the resale value of a model that many considered undervalued.

What makes some instruments more desirable or more in fashion is a cyclical process, in part due to which models

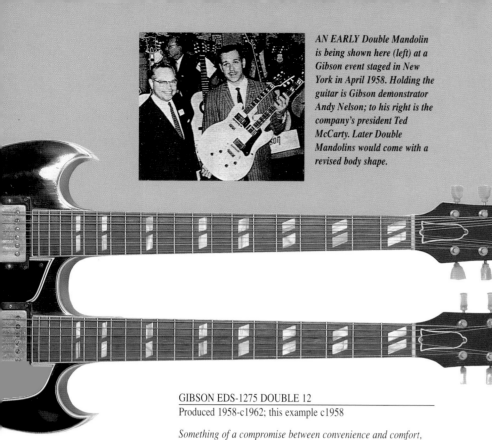

AN EARLY Double Mandolin is being shown here (left) at a Gibson event staged in New York in April 1958. Holding the guitar is Gibson demonstrator Andy Nelson; to his right is the company's president Ted McCarty. Later Double Mandolins would come with a revised body shape.

GIBSON EDS-1275 DOUBLE 12
Produced 1958-c1962; this example c1958

Something of a compromise between convenience and comfort, the twin-neck guitar found its way into Gibson's line in 1958 in the shape of the semi-hollow EDS instruments ('Electric Double Spanish'). The special-order guitars were made with a carved spruce top on a maple body, and a pair of mahogany necks.

GIBSON offered two twin-neck models (shown in the 1960 catalog, above). The Double 12 (left) mixed 12-string and six-string necks, while the Double Mandolin (right) had a standard six-string plus a short-scale six-string neck tuned an octave higher than normal. Gibson's special-order twin-necks came in solidbody style from 1962.

MOST EXPLORERS have a long, drooping headstock rather than this V-shape head (right).

◁ GIBSON EXPLORER
Produced 1958-1959, various re-issues; this example 1958

Gibson's Explorer found even less favor when it was launched in 1958 than its companion Modernistic guitar, the Flying V. While factory records are not entirely clear, the best estimates put the original 1958-59 Explorer production at 22 units, with a further 16 assembled from leftover parts in the early 1960s.

GIBSON's move to weird shapes in 1958 influenced other makers to loosen up at the drawing board. Kay's Solo King (below, and in 1960 catalog, right) in single-pickup guise was less than a third of the price of Gibson's Modernistic axes, and twice as ugly. Kay optimistically described the Solo King as "compact, easy to hold".

△ KAY SOLO KING
Produced 1958-1960; this example c1958

As if to prove that anything Gibson can do Kay can do worse, the Solo King was Kay's attempt to jump the weird-shape bandwagon. Wisely, they jumped off again very quickly.

are being used by musicians who are currently famous. The 1970s are considered by many to be a time of 'death by keyboard' (you know, disco – rhythm & blues for people who have neither). Most of the major manufacturers were sleepwalking through their own production processes. This general lack of attention to detail and corporate complacency made guitarists long for products constructed at the same quality level as the 'originals'. For most players and collectors, this would mean that they had to look for vintage instruments: the genuine articles.

So what is it that makes a 'vintage' instrument a 'collectible'? It is more than its being good sounding and having great playability. It is rarity, originality and condition. Lest we overstress this concept, the difference between (1) a completely original 1954 Strat in near mint

GIBSON's 335 appeared to be a hollow-body thinline guitar, but it effectively combined a hollow-body guitar with a solidbody by incorporating a solid block of maple running from neck to strap button through the center of an otherwise hollow body. This made the guitar much less prone to the screeching feedback that afflicted many hollow-body electrics when played at high volume.

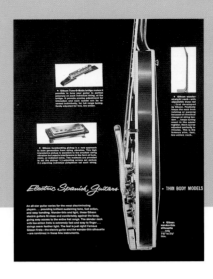

GIBSON's thinline body style (explained in this 1960 catalog feature, left) was by 1958 used on five instruments: the Byrdland, ES-350T, 335TD, 225T and 125T. That same year the company also had five full-depth electric hollow-body guitars in the line: the Super 400CES, L-5CES, ES-5 Switchmaster, ES-295, and the ES-175.

△ GIBSON ES-335TDN
Produced 1958-1960; this example October 1959

The 'dot-neck 335' has become a prime collectible guitar. The original production of the ES-335TD with dot-shape fingerboard markers lasted only from 1958 to 1962, when Gibson replaced the dots with block-shape markers. The earliest 335 models were officially named ES-335T (the T stands for 'thinline') but soon a D was added by Gibson (D means 'double' pickups). The extra N on the model shown stands for 'natural' finish; ES-335TD alone indicates the sunburst variety. From 1960 the 335 was also available in a cherry red finish, known as an ES-335TDC.

COLLECTORS prefer 335s with 'dot' necks, but also with 'long' pickguards that extend beyond the bridge (as on all the 335s shown here), a type used until late in 1960. Early the following year a shorter pickguard that stopped level with the bridge was adopted.

DESIGN PAT. NO. 181,867

Gibson ES-335T

The newest star in a long list of Gibson favorites, this revolutionary new double cutaway, thin electric Spanish guitar meets today's needs for individual performance, large or small ensembles, recording, television and radio. Engineered after consultation with leading players, the ES-335T presents a striking appearance and sensational response. New body construction, with solid fitting neck, pickups and adjustable bridge, provides the solidity essential for clear, sparkling, sustaining tone—while retaining a body size and shape that is easy and comfortable to hold. Provides easy access throughout the entire twenty-two fret range on all six strings.

The double cutaway, thin body, with arched top and back of curly maple has matching maple rims and pearloid binding • extra narrow, slim Honduras mahogany neck with Gibson Adjustable Truss Rod • attractive peghead with large pearl inlays • Rosewood fingerboard with pearl dot inlays • twin, humbucking pickups located for contrasting treble and bass response • individually adjustable polepieces • separate tone and volume controls which can be preset • toggle switch to activate either or both pickups • Tune-O-Matic bridge permits adjustment of string action and individual string length for perfect intonation • nickel plated metal parts • enclosed individual machine heads with deluxe buttons.

SPECIFICATIONS
16" wide, 19" long, 1¾" thick, 24¾" scale, 22 frets
ES-335TN—Natural Finish................................$282.50
ES-335T—Sunburst Finish................................267.50
No. 519 Case—Faultless, plush lined.................46.50

△ GIBSON ES-335TD
Produced 1958-current; this example September 1959

The sunburst 335 was always made in greater numbers than the natural version, which was dropped in 1960. For example, in 1959 Gibson shipped 521 sunburst but only 71 natural 335s.

THE 335 was Gibson's first thinline model to feature a pair of symmetrical cutaways (left) for easier high-note playing.

MANY GIBSON ES thinline models feature this so-called 'crown' inlay on the headstock (above right), although the

ES-355, for example, boasts a split diamond, while the ES-330 has a plain head with only the Gibson logo.

△ GIBSON ES-335TDN
Produced 1958-1960; this example November 1959

When a Bigsby vibrato was factory-fitted, tailpiece holes were covered with pearl (as here) or a black 'Custom Made' plate.

condition with original form-fit brown case and 'tags' (meaning warranty, and other manufacturers' informative blurbs), strap, cord and key to the case, and (2) a refretted '54 Strat with one non-original pickup and the Bakelite replaced with more modern plastic, can be a loss of 50 per cent of its value. And if the instrument has also at some stage been 'refinished' – in other words if the original finish has been replaced – then the guitar will be worth even less on the vintage market.

The one exception to the general rule of all collectibles is the flame-driven market of the original Les Paul Sunburst, or 'Standard'. In this singular instance a highly tiger-striped example with a repaired headstock and new tuners can still fetch its maximum potential, while a Plain Jane with virtually no 'figure' (the visible pattern) but in clean original condition will be worth 30 to 40 per cent less. We marvel at the forgiving myopia of the Les Paul collector in allowing for such a lapse in condition when searching for the eternal flame.

The custom-color phenomenon of Fender guitars asserts the primacy of the iconographic value of a custom paint job in ways which were never realized in the automotive market. A rare, cool custom color such as fiesta red or shoreline gold, or the 'Mary Kaye' combination of transparent blonde with gold hardware, dramatically enhances the price of a Stratocaster so equipped. When one perceives these factors as having discernible market value it becomes readily apparent that the vintage guitars under discussion have a representational and artistic worth that goes beyond what they are as functional objects. This, in essence, is exactly what qualifies them as 'collectible'.

The guitar industry has sought, today, to internalize this phenomenon in creating "collectors' edition" guitars and limited runs of guitars with specific appointments. In most instances these are produced in larger quantities in one year than many of the original vintage instruments were made during their entire production runs. But this phenomenon has had a laudable side effect in that it has caused the major manufacturers to re-examine the construction of their own vintage guitars and to at least attempt to reproduce in contemporary instruments the qualities which made the originals great.

We cannot go back in time like Michael J Fox did in his De Lorean, but we can still own the beloved artifacts of the past. Part of the beauty of the vintage guitar is that these old instruments continue to be playable, so that we can still create new music from old technology. Guitars as collectibles have taken on a life of their own (would that we could, also). With their great increase in value, some guitars are no longer suitable to drag to the local bar to play the Friday night gig, as much as we might like to. While many may bemoan the state of affairs, arguing that guitars are made to be played, the fact that collector-grade instruments will be preserved in glass-walled aggregations means that this musical heritage will, at least partially, be preserved for our descendants.

On the other hand, as long as there are mirrors and electric guitars, flea markets and pawn shops on the secondary roads, and accepting spouses and local taverns, there will be weekend warriors who preserve the rock'n'roll culture of the 1950s. ■ STAN JAY & LARRY WEXER

RADIO & TELEVISION *by Michael Wright*

In the warm glow of memory, radio and television in the 1950s have an image of being innocent Happy Days, of Ricky Ricardo yelling "Lu – cy!" or Sheb Wooley singing about the Purple People Eater. But with the emergence of radio and television as primary vehicles of entertainment, the reality was much more turbulent, involving inter-media struggle and inter-generational strife. Often, an electric guitar would hover somewhere near the center of that controversy.

TV WAS invented in the 1920s, but it wasn't until the 1939 New York World's Fair that the medium really caught the imagination of the American people. In 1946, NBC established the first TV network, and by the end of the 1940s there were four competing US networks: NBC, CBS, ABC and DuMont. Television was instantaneously

successful, and by 1956 more than 70 per cent of all US homes had TVs. For most of the first half of the 1950s, when ads like this (above) appeared, US television programming was essentially a transference of 1940s radio to the new medium, with variety shows, quiz shows, crime dramas and comedies being taken straight off the radio.

CONTROLS (below) are a volume for each pickup and overall tone (although a volume knob is missing here).

RADIO & TELEVISION

As the 1950s began, the medium of television was doing its best to kill radio. Commercial radio broadcasting had been around in the US since the early 1920s, with the big networks NBC and CBS forming in 1926. From the early days on, radio thrived as a live medium, with live variety shows and big orchestras. However, big changes in taste occurred after 1945, as war-weary citizens settled into suburban domesticity and began to create the baby boom. Radio audiences preferred to hear quiz shows and dramatic productions: Gangbusters, The Lone Ranger, and I Love Lucy. Instead of big bands, listeners favored singers. National radio networks were becoming fiscal dinosaurs. As a result they started to look for new outlets, and where they looked was television.

Guitars had a presence on 1950s television programming, but except for a few big highlights their role was limited. Actually, two guitarists had their own network shows just as the decade dawned. Folk singer Paul Arnold hosted American Song in 1948, and later a folk and country program The Paul Arnold Show which lasted until 1950, while tenor jazz guitarist Eddie Condon hosted Eddie Condon's Floor Show into 1950.

One of the longest running of the new variety shows that also debuted in 1948 was The Perry Como Show, which frequently featured Les Paul and Mary Ford. It was undoubtedly this exposure which helped propel the duo to superstardom, leading in 1953 to their own daily five-minute Les Paul & Mary Ford Show

sponsored by Listerine, although after that year's No.1 summer smash, 'Vaya Con Dios', which stayed on the chart for 31 weeks, the brilliant guitarist's sun would set far faster than it had risen.

Perhaps the biggest and most influential of the early variety shows were Arthur Godfrey's Talent Scouts (1948) and Arthur Godfrey And His Friends (1949), which led the ratings and introduced many new artists to the public, including Roy Clark (although both Elvis and Buddy Holly would fail to succeed at auditions for Godfrey).

Indeed, as an illustration of the power of this new medium, it was Godfrey who almost single-handedly started the craze for ukuleles. Godfrey, between sips of Lipton tea, would occasionally strum a uke and, in fact, actually had an instructional TV show in 1950. When Godfrey discovered an inexpensive but good plastic uke and promoted it on his show, he sparked a run on plastic instruments designed and made by the great Mario Maccaferri. Countless little baby boomers started playing ukes. For many, this led to a lifelong addiction to guitars.

Another form of the variety show that came from radio days involved Country & Western music. These shows were generally full of corn-pone humor and lots of guitar-based music. An almost endless stream of country shows began in 1949 with the ABC Barn Dance (featuring the Sage Riders) followed by 1951's Midwestern Hayride out of Dayton (with steel ace Jerry Byrd), 1952's The Eddy Arnold Show (with Chet Atkins), 1955's Grand Ole Opry, Cleveland's Pee Wee King Show, Ozark Jubilee (starring

BODIES and necks for Guyatone's solidbody guitars were manufactured by Maruha Musical Instruments in Kyushu and assembled in Guyatone's Tokyo factory.

MAGNA Electronics began making Magnatone amplifiers in the late 1940s, adding solidbody electric guitars to the line in 1956. Based in California, Magna found that its guitars were never as popular as its amplifiers, of which Buddy Holly was the most famous 1950s user.

...don't
bug me
baby...

...I've switched to MAGNATONE

MAGNA's first Magnatone guitars appeared in 1956. Assistance came from fellow Californian Paul Bigsby, who provided hardware for several models, including the Mark V of 1957. A new Rickenbacker-like line was launched in 1959 when ex-Rickenbacker man Paul Barth briefly came on board. The Magnatone brand lasted into the 1960s, also used on organs and hi-fi gear.

△ MAGNATONE MARK V
Produced 1957-1960; this example c1959

As well as the obvious vibrato, the pickups and control panel are typical of the work of Magna's collaborator Paul Bigsby.

▷ MAGNATONE MARK III DELUXE
Produced c1957-1960; this example c1958

A typical budget concoction of the 1950s: note the enormous Formica pickguard covering the whole of the front, the Bakelite knobs, and the unmistakable 'M' logo on the tailpiece.

▽ GUYATONE LG-30
Produced c1958-c1963; this example c1959

Exported from Japan under Guyatone and Antoria brandnames, models such as this were staples of the British beat scene of the late 1950s and early 1960s, being cheap, electric and available.

HEADSTOCKS might be plain (above right) or bear a brandname logo (below).

GUYATONE

SOLID
Electric
GUITARS

Unexcelled Value- Quality- Performance

DESPITE the presence of a truss-rod cover on the headstock (right), the LG60B's truss-rod was not adjustable.

△ GUYATONE LG-60B
Produced c1958-c1963; this example c1958

Guyatone in Japan enjoyed clear US influences on its first solidbody electrics: the LG of the model name stands for Les Paul Guitar, while the body shape was in fact influenced by 1950s Supro models such as the Belmont (made by Valco in Chicago). Guyatone's LGs, developed around 1958 for export, soon featured Fender-style heads with six-in-a-line tuners.

BRITISH Guyatone distributor J&I Arbiter issued this leaflet (above) in 1959. It showed an LG-50 (£25), and listed LG-30 (£20) and LG-60 (£30) models.

RICKY SINGS AGAIN

One hour before show time

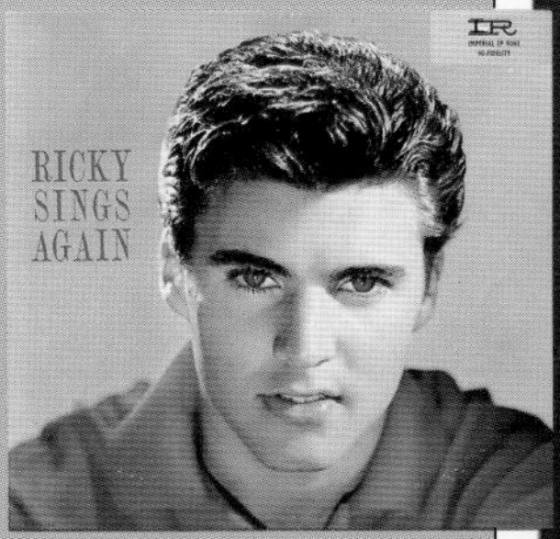

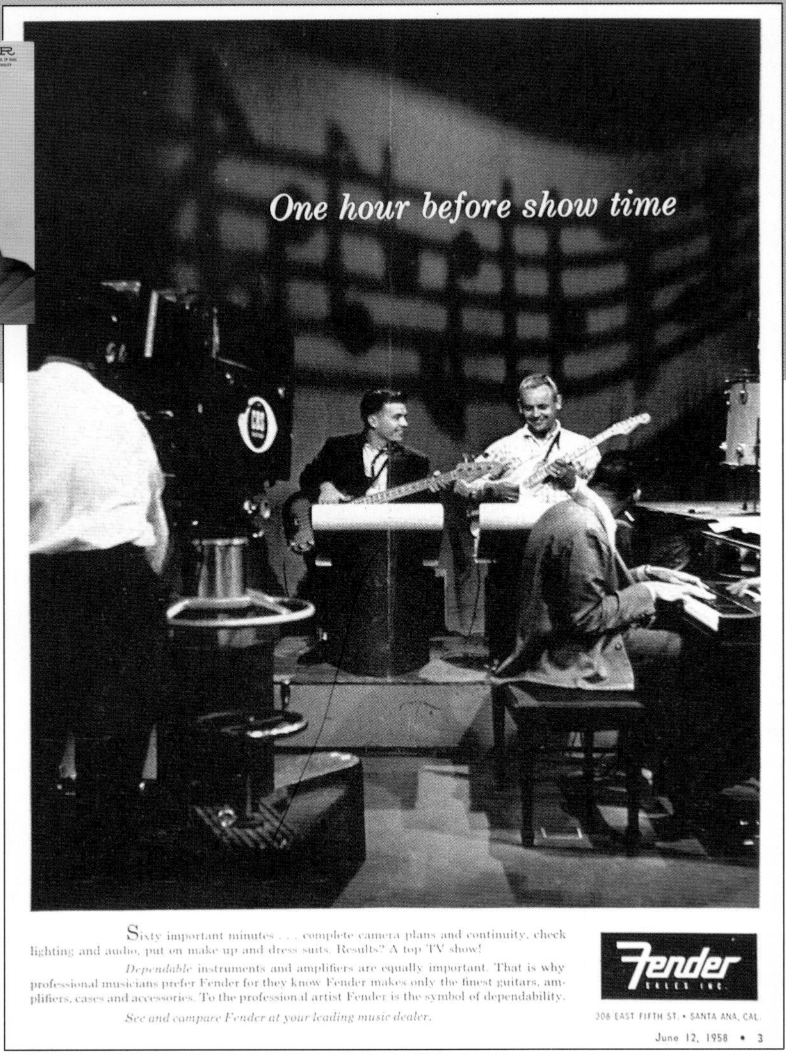

Red Foley and featuring Hank Garland's 'Sugarfoot Rag'), 1956's The Ford Show with the peapicker Tennessee Ernie Ford, 1957's The Jimmie Dean Show (from Washington DC, featuring Johnny Cash), and 1959's The Jimmie Rodgers Show. All flashed guitars on to the television screen and highlighted the work of hot pickers.

Less serious but no less influential were a number of cowboy shows which transferred from radio, including children's Western adventures such as The Gene Autry Show which bowed in 1950 and featured Ray Whitley's classic 'Back In The Saddle Again' as a theme song. A year later The Roy Rogers Show began, with plenty of wholesome guitar interludes.

While people were beginning to see more guitars on TV, most often either acoustic or electric archtops, radio – remember radio? – was preparing a counter-assault in America that would make absolutely sure folks heard guitars, and change the course of known civilization.

FENDER instruments are promoted in a CBS TV studio setting in this 1958 ad (right). No doubt the ad agency were pleased with the coup of placing Fender in the studio of one of the leading American TV networks of the day. But ironically it was CBS who, just seven years later, would buy out the Fender companies in a spectacular deal that would see $13 million change hands.

GRETSCH's Country Club Stereo was available in Cadillac green (below) or normal sunburst finish.

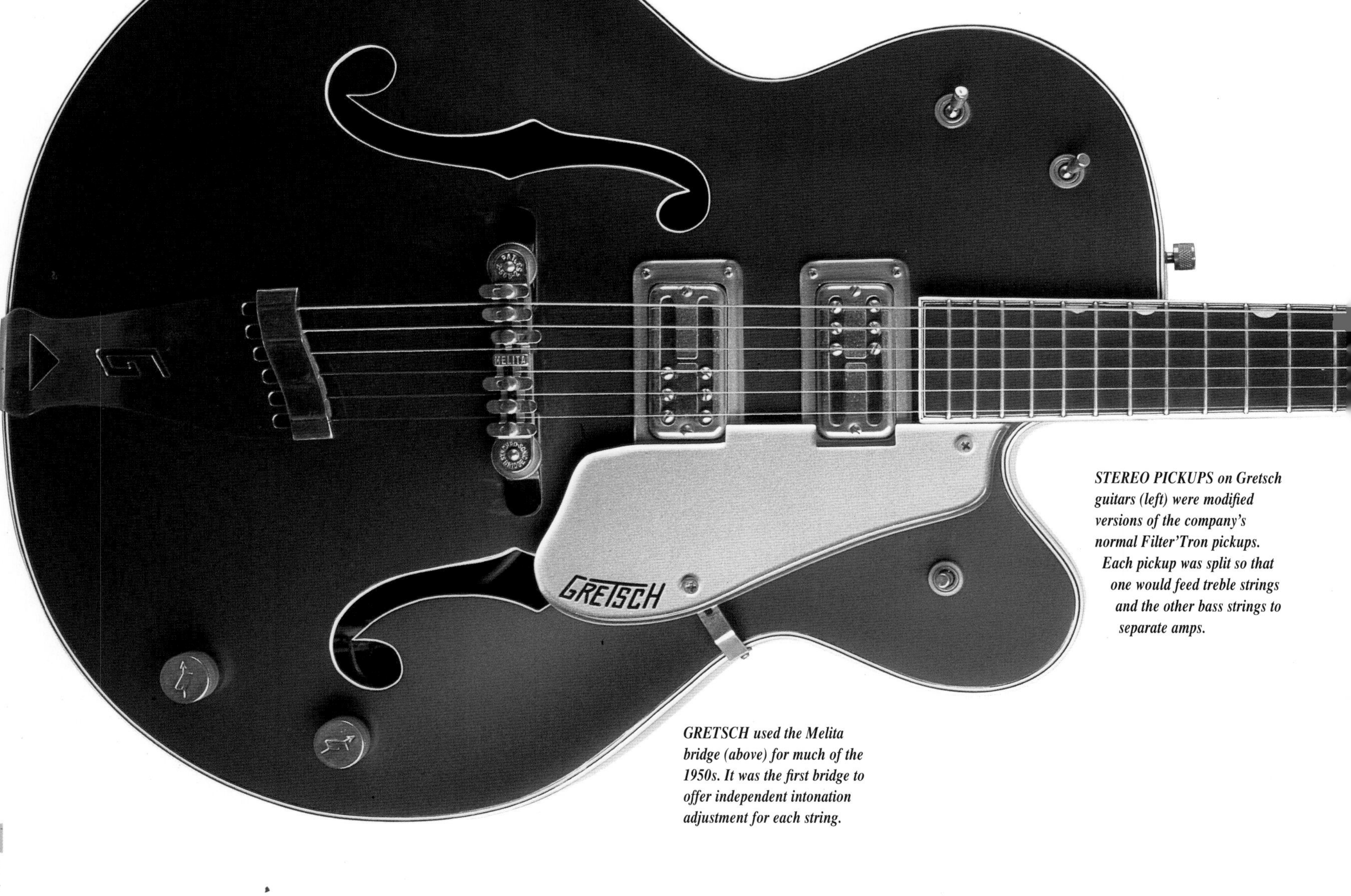

STEREO PICKUPS on Gretsch guitars (left) were modified versions of the company's normal Filter'Tron pickups. Each pickup was split so that one would feed treble strings and the other bass strings to separate amps.

GRETSCH used the Melita bridge (above) for much of the 1950s. It was the first bridge to offer independent intonation adjustment for each string.

72

GUITARS *appeared in many unexpected places on American TV of the 1950s. In 1955, The Lawrence Welk Show hit the air to almost universal critical scorn. A relic of the accordion craze that was already over by the time it aired, Welk's show did nonetheless feature solos by (smiling) guitarist Buddy Merrill. Sessionman and* Gibson *endorser Tony Mottola made 'original descriptive music' for something called* Danger *(right). Even Desi Arnaz would occasionally strum an ax for bits of I Love Lucy. And who could forget Jane Davies on the Ina Ray Hutton Show, or Jimmy Dodd picking a rodent-shaped guitar on The Mickey Mouse Club?*

Back when the US networks divested themselves of radio, a number of developments began to coalesce which would redefine the medium and eventually re-establish its cultural importance. For one thing, in the late 1940s American radio stations increasingly relied on recorded music to replace the disappearing network programming. In 1949 Todd Storz, owner of KOWH in Omaha, Nebraska, invented the Top 40 radio format, playing the most popular tunes in rotation. The idea swept the radio industry like wildfire. In around 1950, New York's WNEW was the first to mix recorded music with news. Radio was ready to find its modern voice.

Simultaneously, momentous changes in music began to occur, for which radio provided the ideal outlet. In 1948, losing money hand over fist, WDIA in Memphis, Tennessee, made a desperate decision and became the first-ever all-black format radio station. They hired a young guitarist to perform, who became known as Blues Boy King. In 1950, not far from WDIA, Sam Phillips opened Sun Studios. That same year WDIA's B.B. King had a national R&B hit with 'Three

DISC JOCKEYS (right) came to personify the shift of emphasis that started during the 1950s from live music performance to the broadcasting of records.

o'clock Blues'. A local young truck driver was listening. His name was Elvis. Meanwhile up in Cleveland, Ohio, in 1951 a disc jockey named Alan Freed began to notice that kids were buying so-called 'race' records – a record business term for uptempo R&B songs by black artists – with a beat they could dance to. The records featured electric guitars.

Freed started playing this music on his show and called it 'rock and roll'. All the kids started listening, and of course the radio business noted the ensuing buzz. In 1954, Freed was hired by New York's WINS to do Alan Freed's Rock & Roll Party. WINS quickly led the New York radio pack, and the rest of radio followed.

The older generation reacted with fear and trembling to the arrival of rock'n'roll. Radio stations were besieged with callers demanding that the 'nigger music' be stopped, or pointing to a Communist conspiracy. The kids just kept buying it up. In 1956 the Memphis truck driver Elvis Presley, backed by Scotty Moore's archtop

electric, copped three No.1 hits. Rock and its electric guitars never looked back, and by 1958 the US Top 40 was dominated by rock'n'roll.

Which brings us back to television – remember television? With American radio fomenting a revolution starring guitar-toting teen idols, TV couldn't ignore the top of the pops. Ironically, it was two stalwarts of the big band era, Tommy and Jimmy Dorsey, who gave the new music one of its early breaks. It was on their program Stage Show that Elvis made his TV debut in January 1956, hips swiveling, many months before his more famous appearances on The Ed Sullivan Show when the camera pulled back to censor his dance in 'Ready Teddy'.

The controversy surrounding Elvis' TV performances turned out to be a tempest in a teapot. Television never did fully warm up to rock'n'roll in the 1950s, and really didn't have to. By the later 1950s, tastes had shifted again and musical variety shows began to give way to Westerns.

Electric guitars show up on a few more American TV programmes in later years, including four shows that were produced during 1957 by Alan Freed, called The Big Beat, with Chuck Berry and Mickey (Baker) & Sylvia, as well as 1959's The Music Shop, with Ritchie Valens.

The decade itself was winding down, and was about to enter the radio 'payola' scandals (which would end Freed's career) and the swinging sixties. But it was the 1950s which laid the foundation, bringing the sounds of electric guitars on to the radio and those censored, swiveling hips on to the television. ■ MICHAEL WRIGHT

GRETSCH COUNTRY CLUB STEREO
Produced 1958-1965; this example 1958

'Stereo' became a magical word in the late 1950s. Pre-recorded stereo tapes first appeared in 1956, LPs a few years later, and in 1958 the first stereo guitars were launched: the Gretsch Country Club Stereo and White Falcon Stereo. They worked by splitting the output of the strings and feeding them to two separate amplifiers.

JIMMIE WEBSTER (right) was Gretsch's guitar ideas man, and he's pictured here with the stereo guitar system he developed for them in 1958.

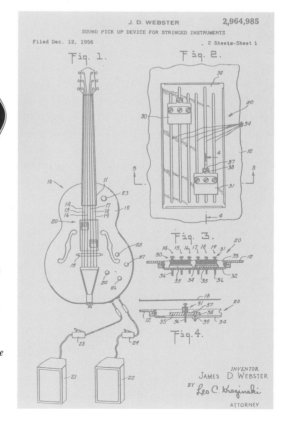

WEBSTER's original patent (right) for the first practical stereo guitar system, filed in 1956, shows a stylized drawing of a large pickup with two individual elements positioned on sliders. In fact, the type put into production had two static, modified pickups, sensing either the three highest or three lowest strings, "whereby tones produced from each of said groups of strings may be selectively controlled".

THE COMPANY which made Rickenbacker guitars was the Electro String Instrument Corporation, formed in Los Angeles in 1934. In 1953 founder Adolph Rickenbacker sold Electro String to businessman F.C. Hall. The following year Rickenbacker's first conventionally shaped electrics began to appear, and in 1958 the classic Capri style (left) hit the market.

▽ RICKENBACKER 360
Produced 1958-current; this example 1959

Rickenbacker introduced a series of models during 1958 that formed the basis for the company's success during the 1960s. These thinline hollow-body electric guitars, known for the first few years as the Capri series, were largely the responsibility of Roger Rossmeisl, an inspired German-born guitar designer and maker who had come to work for Rickenbacker around 1954.

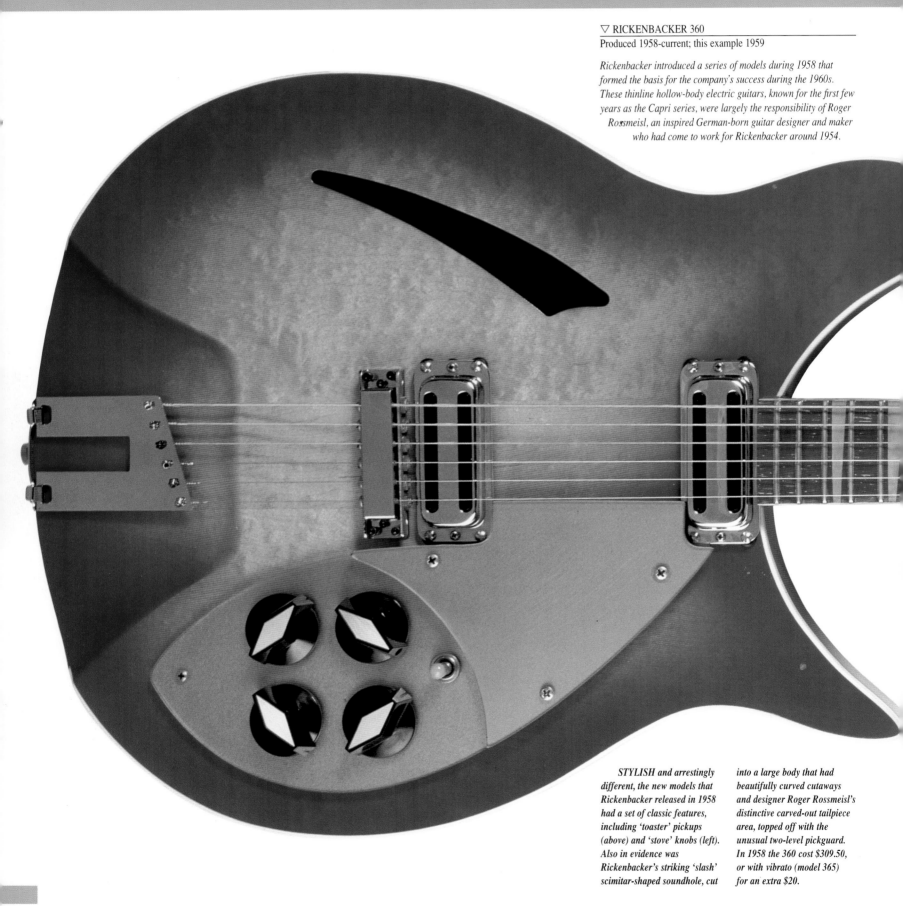

STYLISH and arrestingly different, the new models that Rickenbacker released in 1958 had a set of classic features, including 'toaster' pickups (above) and 'stove' knobs (left). Also in evidence was Rickenbacker's striking 'slash' scimitar-shaped soundhole, cut into a large body that had beautifully curved cutaways and designer Roger Rossmeisl's distinctive carved-out tailpiece area, topped off with the unusual two-level pickguard. In 1958 the 360 cost $309.50 or with vibrato (model 365) for an extra $20.

RECORDING *by John Morrish*

At the start of the 1950s recording was still a primitive affair. Disc-cutting was still preferred to tape recording. By the end of the decade, however, the disc-cutting machines had been banished, the first eight-track machines were in limited use and stereo was becoming the norm. But the decade also saw an important change in the role of the people doing the recording, who started as white-coated technicians and ended as participants in the artistic process.

METRONOME
MUSIC USA SEPTEMBER, 1957 35¢

RECORDING

Tape recording was born in Germany in 1935 when AEG demonstrated a prototype machine, which was quickly subsumed into the German war effort. After the war, the allies were shocked to discover that magnetic tape recorders had been used to record their radio transmissions for decoding.

As part of the spoils of war, the magnetic tape machines were brought back to Britain and America and shamelessly copied. By 1946 the Ampex corporation of America was able to supply broadcasters with equipment to record radio shows for subsequent rebroadcast. Recording studios acquired their first tape machines in 1947, using a single channel on ¼in tape. Even so, as late as 1952 engineers still argued that lacquer discs provided a higher quality recording medium, as well as a more durable and permanent record. This is not so ludicrous as it sounds: early tape was mechanically unstable and suffered from the problem of 'print-through', whereby the magnetic pattern in one length of

tape was picked up by the piece of tape wound underneath it, producing audible 'pre-echo' and 'post-echo' during quiet patches or between tracks.

At the same time, engineers began to see tape's inherent advantages. "Many clients prefer to use tape, even though the cost for a given program time is considerably higher – largely because changes and corrections can be made so easily after the recording," said one studio chief in 1952.

The early 1950s were a time of rising commercial confidence, and major record companies such as Capitol Records invested in new facilities where, with extremely limited equipment available for the electronic manipulation of sound, great efforts were made to ensure that the initial recorded sound was as clear as possible.

The creation of tape machines with separate record and playback heads from 1951 meant that for the first time recordings could be monitored 'off-tape' as they happened. This not only prevented ruinous mistakes but also ended the quality compromise inherent in using the same head both to record and to play back. Mixers were modified to

MAGNETIC recording had been demonstrated at the end of the 19th century, but for commercial purposes the mechanical method, inscribing vibrations into wax discs or cylinders, remained dominant. In the 1920s electrical microphones, mixers and cutting lathes improved matters greatly, and

better aluminum foil and acrylic discs arrived in the late 1940s. But recording remained a one-shot affair: the sound made in the studio was recorded on the disc, and no later alteration was possible. Magnetic recording, initially on wire, was generally restricted to telegraphic and office dictation purposes, and tape recorders did not come into wide use in studios until the 1950s.

RICKENBACKER's 360/365 and 370/375 models came with these triangle markers (below).

DANELECTRO moved to a new lyre-shaped 'Long Horn' design in 1958, and this ad from the following year (right) shows the Guitarlin in the new style, as well as a double-neck guitar-and-bass combination with the less outrageous 'Short Horn' body shape. Danelectro founder Nathan Daniel explained the Long Horn shape: "The idea was simply to give the player as much access as possible, which meant we had a deep cutaway on both sides. It did make an unusual look, sure. But it was an unusual name too: a couple of long horns!"

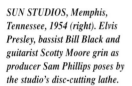

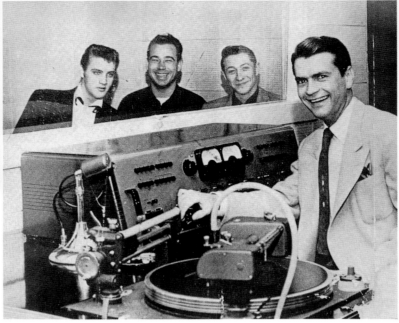

SUN STUDIOS, Memphis, Tennessee, 1954 (right). Elvis Presley, bassist Bill Black and guitarist Scotty Moore grin as producer Sam Phillips poses by the studio's disc-cutting lathe.

songwriters and producers Leiber & Stoller and Atlantic's chief engineer Tom Dowd, working with The Coasters in New York. But the spread of multitrack was not universal. The Beatles used only two-track — voices on one channel, instruments on the other — as late as 1963.

The frequency range and balance captured by the best studios in the 1950s was little different than that boasted by modern facilities, at least until the invention of digital recording. The sheer simplicity of the methods used, straight from microphone to tape with a minimum of processing, was capable of producing sounds of

breathtaking realism and presence. Only in the high levels of ambient noise (which were an inevitable consequence of the tube electronics employed) do some of these recordings betray their age.

But while the major studios were capable of technical excellence, they were not at the forefront of musical developments. The 1950s saw the rise of independent recording labels and small studios which were ideally placed to discover and record new types of music. These studios were often run by a single engineer and/or proprietor, and would survive from week to week by

recording mundane local events, while using the income generated to subsidize their real musical interests.

Sam Phillips's Memphis Recording Service, better known as the Sun studios where Elvis Presley made his first records, was typical. Sun had a single recording room 18ft by 30ft, with a control room at one end and an office at the other. Phillips had no more than eight microphones and a five-into-one mixing desk. And he had a pair of Presto disc-cutting lathes, one of which made the first known recording of Elvis Presley who called at the studio to make a demo, ostensibly to play to his mother.

Phillips also had two good Ampex tape machines, the second of which was used to provide the primitive 'slapback' echo that is the Sun recordings' trademark. A feed was taken to the machine, probably from a microphone in the recording room: its placement would account for the way the effect varies from track to track. Once recorded, it was immediately picked up off the monitor head and fed back into the final mix: the delay inherent in this process created the initial echo. With

ANDY NELSON (left), described as Gibson's "artist-enthusiast", poses with a mono ES-355 in this 1959 ad. Gibson offered the 355 in mono and stereo formats, the mono variety also lacking a Varitone control. As the 355 continued in production during the 1960s, Gibson produced more stereo than mono models.

▽ GIBSON LES PAUL SPECIAL
Produced 1955-1959, various re-issues; this example 1959

After a weakness was revealed at the neck/body joint, later examples have the neck pickup moved further down the body.

MODEL STEREO
ES345T -N
A31383
PRICE $444 5°
w/case
GUARANTEE

Your Gibson guitar is guaranteed against defects in workmanship or materials. Service necessitated by ordinary wear, accident, or by negligence and adverse climatic conditions are excepted. Transportation charges involved in shipment both ways to be paid by purchaser.

GIBSON, INC., KALAMAZOO, MICHIGAN

FOR TOP PERFORMANCE OF YOUR NEW GIBSON

STEREO was a buzz word in the late 1950s not only in studios but also with guitar makers.

Gibson's ES-345 (below) was its first stereo guitar, as proudly stamped on the tag (left) that came with this instrument.

▷ GIBSON ES-345TDN

Produced 1959-1981; this example October 1959

After Gretsch had introduced the first stereo guitar in 1958 (see p72), Gibson came up with a simpler stereo system for its ES-345 and 355 models which sends each pickup to separate amps.

CHERRY RED (below) was the color in which most ES-355s were finished, apart from a few *custom jobs, until a walnut option was offered by Gibson in the late 1960s.*

△ GIBSON ES-355TD-SV

Produced 1959-1981; this example November 1959

Gibson's ES-355 was a deluxe version of the 335, and the SV suffix of this example identifies it as a stereo model with Varitone. The large Varitone control, developed by Gibson's pickup expert Walt Fuller, is situated above the usual knobs, and is used to select from six preset tonal settings. It proved unpopular with players and is often disconnected.

GIBSON STEREO

TONY MOTTOLA (left) demos a stereo ES-355 through Gibson's GA-88S stereo amp outfit "enabling the guitarist to create a symphony of warm, full stereophonic sound".

FIVE FEET OF LOVIN' · THE WAYWARD WIND
SOMEBODY HELP ME · KEEP IT A SECRET

PART **1**
EAP1-1059

Capitol
RECORDS

HIGH FIDELITY
RECORDING

THE CAPITOL TOWER,
HOLLYWOOD

a gene vincent record date
WITH THE BLUE CAPS

accommodate off-tape monitoring as well as the output of the desk. Monitor speakers usually derived from cinema sound systems and, particularly in the US, used horn tweeters. Even in the 1950s, records were monitored at extremely high levels.

Tape machines developed for the defense industry were capable of recording several tracks across the same tape. As early as 1947, experimental stereo recording on two and three channels had been shown, but it was not until 1953 that the first commercial stereo recorders were available from Ampex and Magnecord. These, particularly the three-track version, rapidly became the studio norm, even for mono. The three tracks enabled vocals or solo instruments to be kept separate until the mix.

In the single-track days, overdubbing had been handled simply by copying from one tape machine to another, adding new instrumentation at the same time. There was an inevitable loss of sound quality each time. Interestingly, the first multitrack recorders, designed for stereo, did not include either 'sound-on-sound' or 'sel-sync'. Sound-on-sound permitted the sound from one track to be added with live material and then be recorded back on to another: this was in effect a more economical form of the old two-machine technique, but the losses were high.

Sel-sync, an abbreviation of 'selective synchronization', introduced as an option during 1956, is the key to modern multitracking. It involves using one channel's record head as a playback head while recording on another: it means that the performer can listen to a previously recorded backing and record his own line in exact synchronization with it. Once sel-sync had become standard equipment, true multitrack was on its way. The first eight-track machines were being used as early as 1958 by the

DURING THE 1950s stereo was gradually establishing itself. The Capitol studio (where Gene Vincent is working, above) was built in 1957 for mono working, but with stereo in mind: initially it was equipped with a 10-channel mixing desk feeding a mono recorder. Also in the 1950s, studios for popular music were designed to keep natural reverberation to a minimum, adding it later by

various controllable means. Principally that meant the echo chamber, a sound-reflective room to which the sound in the studio could be sent and then picked up by a microphone and fed back into the mix. Capitol had no fewer than four underground echo chambers. Efforts were also made to isolate the recording rooms from their surroundings by a system of air gaps and floors 'floating' on cork.

RICKENBACKER's effective 'underlined' logo (above) had begun to appear on the company's first modern electric models launched in 1954. The distinctive curved, pointed

plate on which it appears was the work of Rickenbacker owner F.C. Hall's wife, Lydia, who cut out paper models until she arrived at the unique shape, still in use today.

DANELECTRO started business in Red Bank, New Jersey, in 1948 as an amp maker, adding guitars in the mid-1950s. By 1959 it had outgrown its old premises, and this stylized drawing from the company's 1959 catalog shows the new Danelectro factory in nearby Neptune.

△ DANELECTRO LONG HORN MODEL 4623
Produced 1958-1969; this example 1958

Among Danelectro's innovations was the six-string bass, which was effectively a guitar tuned an octave lower than usual. The best known player of six-string-bass was Duane Eddy, who owns the example shown here; it was used for such classic Eddy tracks as 'Because They're Young', recorded early in 1960.

METRONOME
MUSIC USA
May, 1957   35c

LES PAUL AND MARY FORD IN HI-FI

SPECIAL HI-FIDELITY ISSUE

LES PAUL (at the controls in his home studio, left, with Mary Ford at the microphone) had an eccentric, self-taught grasp of the recording process that inspired some great ideas. While guitarist Paul wasn't the first to use overdubbing, his multi-guitar piece 'Lover', recorded in 1947 and released by Capitol the following year as

Les Paul's 'New Sound', did much to attract attention to the potential of overdubbing, as did his subsequent hits with Ford such as 'How High The Moon'. Later, Paul came up with the avant-garde idea of an eight-track tape recorder, and commissioned the Ampex company to build him the very first such machine in 1957.

rock'n'roll, eagerly copied at hundreds of small studios across the country. Independent engineers were expected to take an active part in recording, pushing up the faders to make drumbeats distort for extra impact, fading in and out echo at appropriate points, riding the faders to smooth out uneven vocal performances. At the same time, the rudimentary nature of recording during the 1950s meant that musicians were naturally adept at playing together in small spaces, listening and reacting to one another, and producing a genuine performance.

Phillips used no overdubbing or splicing. Each section of tape produced in the Sun studios represents a single moment in time. Other independent studios and producers were adept at tape editing, often splicing several takes together to make one finished song, and at overdubbing by copying from machine to machine. This clumsy technique was used to great effect on many of Buddy Holly's recordings, starting with 'Words of Love' in spring 1957. The independents undoubtedly led the way in pop, while the majors tried to catch up. ■ JOHN MORRISH

equipment so basic, Phillips' fundamental resource was time itself. While engineers who worked in major studios were tied to rigid session schedules and union agreements, not to mention technical standards and textbook procedures, those in independent studios had the time and freedom for experimentation.

Phillips, for instance, permitted levels of distortion that would not have been acceptable in the large studios of the time. For example, he would place guitar amplifiers in the bathroom to get a harder sound. And he had his famous echo effect. All these things were the lifeblood of early

PLANE CRASH KILLS STARS

NEW YORK, Wednesday.—The world's pop fans were shattered this week by the tragic deaths of three top disc stars—Buddy Holly, Big Bopper (J. P. Richardson) and Ritchie Valens.

BUDDY HOLLY is killed in a plane crash in Iowa along with Ritchie Valens and the Big Bopper.

RUSSIA launches Lunik I into planetary orbit around the sun, lands Lunik II on the moon, and uses Lunik III to take the first photographs of the dark side of the moon.

CALIFORNIA passes the first exhaust emissions law in the United States.

WIZARDRY ON WHEELS

The Revolutionary
MORRIS *Mini-Minor*

BMC's MINI, "the people's car", is launched on the UK market. Designed by Alec Issigonis, the $750 Mini is described by one newspaper as the vehicle "for which tens of thousands of economy motorists have been waiting". Meanwhile the initial section of Britain's first freeway, the MI, is opened for traffic.

IN CUBA, dictator Fulgencio Batista's government is overthrown by a revolutionary movement under Fidel Castro.

THE WORLD's population is estimated at 2800 million, and is said to be increasing at the rate of 45 million every year.

DEAD: Guitar Slim, Cecil B De Mille and Billie Holiday. Born: Richie Sambora, Emma Thompson and Bryan Adams.

SOVIET leader Nikita Kruschev visits the United States; his main complaint is that for security reasons he is not allowed to tour Disneyland. Later he observes: "The people are for peace." Quite right.

▽ GIBSON LES PAUL SPECIAL
Produced 1955-1959, various re-issues; this example 1959

A shortlived variant, the double-cutaway Junior replaced the single-cut version early in '59, and was renamed SG Special later in the year. Only a small number would have been left-handed like this rare example.

GIBSON's Les Paul Special was offered in cherry red (above) for the first time when it changed to the company's new double-cutaway style body in 1959.

EUROPEAN GUITARS *by Paul Day*

In contrast to the United States, Europe in the early 1950s was still deep in the age of post-war austerity, and young people were not yet afforded their own identity nor the luxury of an independent lifestyle. While rock'n'roll was beginning to make waves across the Atlantic, it had yet to have any impact in the UK, where the guitar often literally took a back seat and the electric variety was still far from common.

THIS GOLDEN Hofner from the early 1960s was presented by Hofner to UK guitar star Bert Weedon, who still owns it today. The rectangular control panel was used from 1958.

GOYA (below) was a brand applied to guitars imported into the US by Hershman. From 1959 some were made by Hagstrom in Sweden, with distinctive touches including colorful plastic finishes and multiple control layouts.

EUROPEAN GUITARS

The British skiffle craze of the mid-1950s inspired thousands to take up the guitar, leading to increasing numbers of cheap and cheerful instruments in circulation. From these humble but fun beginnings many aspiring musicians made what seemed to be a natural progression to rock'n'roll. As the new sounds which reflected the fast-changing face of American popular music began to filter across the big pond, so too came a growing awareness that the guitars used on US records must be very different from those found in Britain and the rest of Europe.

Record albums and theater or TV appearances by visiting American artists provided a tantalizing taste of futuristic Fenders, exotic Epiphones, glossy Gibsons, Gretsches or Guilds, and radical Rickenbackers. Despite their undoubted desirability, such tools of this new trade were beyond the reach of most British guitarists, not just financially and

geographically, but also politically, as a 1951 UK government embargo on foreign instrument imports would not be lifted until summer 1959.

So it was that in the 1950s choice and availability remained very limited in Britain, despite the increasing popularity of the instrument. Rock'n'roll was becoming a major player in the music business, with the electric guitar considered de rigueur. Of course, both rock'n'roll and its electric exponents were despised by 'real' musicians, many of whom were nonetheless still required to play this dreaded devil's music on the new instruments – which does much to explain the low standards of British recorded re-creations of contemporary US hits in the 1950s.

The West German maker Hofner assumed a high profile in the UK quite early on, thanks to importer Selmer, at first with electrified big-bodied archtops, then smaller-bodied Club models and, in 1956, its solidbody Colorama. In the

SPOTLIGHT ON *Goya*

WEST GERMAN maker Hofner made a big impact in 1950s Britain, as shown in importer Selmer's 1959 ad (right) that features an eccentric mixture of the top UK bandsmen, session players and embryonic rock'n'rollers.

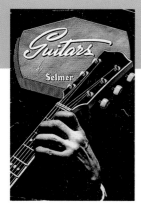

SELMER were the biggest UK importer of electric guitars in the 1950s. The 1957 catalog (above) features a Hofner.

TOMMY STEELE was Britain's first rock'n'roll star, before becoming the dreaded 'all-round entertainer'. His first hit was 'Rock With The Caveman' (1956), and in '57 he made No.1 with 'Singing The Blues'. Steele is pictured (left) with a Hofner Committee and is seen in the big ad (far left) with a Hofner President.

▽ HOFNER GOLDEN HOFNER THIN

Produced 1959-1962; this example 1961

The West German Hofner company added the Golden Hofner model to the top of its line at the end of the 1950s. Described by Hofner as "a masterpiece of guitar perfection", it was certainly the company's most ornate and attractive electric hollow-body guitar. By 1959, as well as an extensive line of domestic-market guitars, Hofner offered nine UK-only models: the Golden Hofner, Committee, President, Senator, Club 40, Club 50 and Club 60 hollow electrics, plus a pair of Colorama solids with one or two pickups.

HOFNER's unique headstock shape (left), used on the Golden Hofner and Committee models, was appropriately described by the company as 'frondose', meaning leaf-like.

HOFNER used some beautiful fingerboard inlays, including the Golden Hofner's pleasing floral pattern (above), bounded by the typically German device of parallel lines.

△ HARMONY STRATOTONE JUPITER H-49

Produced 1959-1965; this example c1960

In the US, Harmony continued to produce electrics such as this Jupiter (in the same line as a Mars and a Mercury model). Controls included a volume and tone per pickup, plus a tone control for the three-way selector's center 'out of phase' position.

HARMONY's colorful catalog of 1958 (above) detailed its competitively priced electric models, ranging from the Mars H-45 at $70 to the Espanada H-63 at $199.50.

infant days of the electric guitar market in the UK such solid 'planks', as they were often derisorily described, were not numerous in comparison to hollow-body electrics. Hofner's original solidbody had few partners in Britain at the time, although one of its first competitors was also handled by an obviously aware Selmer.

The Grazioso solidbody was made by the Neoton company in Prague, Czechoslovakia, an unlikely origin for a guitar so heavily influenced by Fender's still-recent creation, that most ultra-American of all electrics, the super-streamlined Stratocaster. Although clumsy styling guaranteed that it was far from a copy, the Neoton Grazioso came with bolt-on maple neck, two-tone sunburst contoured body, triple pickups, built-in bridge/vibrato unit and a front-recessed output jack. This array of features, strongly suggestive of Fender, guaranteed instant appeal and, accordingly, impressive sales to numerous nascent

pluckers such as George Harrison and Albert Lee. Selmer soon realized that the 'Grazioso' name was uncommercial, and swiftly changed it to the more American-imaged 'Futurama' (see p83).

The late 1950s brought the first Japanese-made electrics to British shores, imported to swell the still thin ranks of solids. These early efforts were primitive and poor in quality, but at least offered an interesting alternative. Most originated from the Tokyo-based Guyatone factory, although these were later imported bearing other logos, including Antoria or Star. Unusually, styling was derived from Valco, a less familiar name on the US solidbody scene and responsible for the National and Supro brands, some models of which featured a single sloping cutaway shape. Guyatone's version employed a smaller body, probably to match the comparatively diminutive stature of Japanese guitarists, and blithely ignored the real needs of a western

export market which was looking for guitars that more closely matched the models made by American companies such as Gibson, Fender, Gretsch and the like.

Despite reductions in dimensions and inherent quality, these oriental imports proved popular in the UK as they certainly embodied a more modern image than many, along with favorably affordable prices. Players such as a young Hank Marvin suffered their shortcomings while awaiting the opportunity to acquire a Fender or Gibson dream machine. Although the former brand certainly took over later as the main influence on guitar design, Gibson's more traditional stance tended to dominate the 1950s.

By the late 1950s the influence of electric guitars had spread worldwide, evidenced by other countries' contributions to the cause, and some of these did make their mark on a pre-beatboom British market. In Sweden, accordion maker Hagstrom decided it wanted a piece of

△ FRAMUS HOLLYWOOD 5/132
Produced 1959-1961; this example c1959

Framus, a German maker, initially dabbled in big hollow-body electrics, entering the solidbody market in 1959. The Hollywood name had an American air, and as the nearest thing to Les Paul lookalikes in Europe at the time they sold well, complete with a choice of one, two or three pickups plus fancy paint jobs.

VEGA's other electrics included the Westerner, shown in this 1959 ad (right). Rusty Draper had a 1950s hit with 'Gambler's Guitar'.

VEGA's control layout for the model 1200 includes a normal volume and tone per pickup (far left), a three-way pickup selector (above the neck) and a two-way selector (left) for mono/stereo operation.

△ VEGA 1200 STEREO
Produced 1959-c1960; this example c1959

In the US, Vega of Boston decided to get themselves noticed in the new stereo scene with this spectacular 12-pickup instrument, which retailed for a steep $1000. "For stereo use with two amplifiers," explained Vega, "a flick of the switch projects all of the treble notes through one amplifier and all the bass notes through the other. Electronic vibrato is also provided."

VEGA's 12 pickups (above) are split into two groups of six, two for each string. The rear six are designed to sense treble tones and the six nearest the neck are for bass response.

SELMER at first imported the Czech-made Futurama (below) bearing its original name of Grazioso, as used by George Harrison in the early days of The Beatles (right).

The NEW! FUTURAMA

The new automatic Futurama is the most revolutionary guitar design in years. Three pick-ups controlled by three simple press buttons give an infinite variety of tones. Vibrato is made easy by the manual tremolo arm. Solid construction from the finest timbers. High gloss sunburst finish. The Futurama leads the way to the future.

55 guineas

THE BEATLES (left) in 1961, as prototype beat-boomers and with pre-fame guitars (left to right): George Harrison with Neoton Grazioso; John Lennon with Hofner Club 40; Paul McCartney, still a guitarist, with Dutch-made Rosetti Solid 7 (ad, below); and Stu Sutcliffe with Hofner 500/5 bass.

NOW! *Rosetti* present the world's best value in ELECTRIC GUITARS

YES! *Lucky 7* **12 gns** COMPLETE

YES! Solid 7 **18 gns** COMPLETE

▽ FUTURAMA 3
Produced 1959-1963; this example c1959

'Futurama' was the brandname that UK importer Selmer applied from around 1959 to the previously-named Grazioso solidbody electric from Czechoslovakian instrument manufacturer Neoton.

SALESMAN Robert Nielsen holds Vega's stereo guitar at its summer 1959 launch (right), as company president William Nelson looks on.

EARLIEST VERSIONS of the Futurama (above) had 'Resonet' on the pickguard,

'Grazioso' on the headstock. Each of the three switches turns a pickup on and off.

the electric guitar action and launched two- and four-pickup solidbody models in 1958. These visually arresting guitars boasted banks of pushbuttons and chromed panels plus abundant sparkle and pearloid plastic – all unsurprisingly appropriate in view of their accordion-derived ancestry. Such exercises in excess even fared well in the US where Hagstroms bore the Goya brandname.

Similar cosmetics would also adorn the offerings from contemporary guitar makers in Italy, as that country countered the dwindling appeal of the accordion by turning to the increasingly popular electric guitar. East Germany and Holland were perhaps less obvious sources, but they too turned out assorted oddballs and budget boxes in the 1950s, while UK makers, although still small in number and size, had not been idle.

Some traditional British brands like Abbott-Victor chose to stay safely staid, but the long-established Grimshaw

company adopted a more adventurous attitude. Its Short-Scale Deluxe model ventured into new stylistic territory, marrying American influences to distinctly English eccentricity. The result was an electric archtop ideal for UK rockers, with teardrop soundholes, curving control panel and innovative six-coil twin pickups. Little wonder that modern-minded players such as Bruce Welch, Joe Brown and Alvin Lee appreciated these advanced-style attributes.

There were virtually no British-built solidbody guitars in the 1950s until Burns-Weill debuted late in the decade. This alliance of Jim Burns and Henry Weill produced a line of solid oddities, some featuring very daring design ideas. In contrast, their Fenton model was afflicted by a small body similar to that found on Japanese electrics, although this was not by accident or coincidence but merely a compliance with UK distributors' requests that Burns-Weill should copy their Far Eastern competitors in terms of size

and shape – a neat twist on future trends. This then was the somewhat restricted electric guitar scene in Britain, until the time when guitarists gained the ultimate freedom of choice. By November 1959 the first official imports of American instruments since the import ban hit UK shores – and the British guitar business would never be the same again. Such competition obviously hit hard at the hitherto insular established brands, but the industry was expanding rapidly as demand for affordable beginner instruments increased in ratio. In the face of this new, long awaited, ultra-attractive opposition, many makers survived and even flourished, often because they were able still to compete on price advantage if not quality.

British guitarists finally had all the options – from basic to best, from frugal to flamboyant – and the future looked rosy for all, manufacturers and music makers alike. The beatboom had begun. ■ PAUL DAY

INDEX

BIBLIOGRAPHY

Chet Atkins *Country Gentleman* (Ballantine 1974).
Tony Bacon & Paul Day *The Fender Book* (IMP/Miller Freeman 1992); *The Gibson Les Paul Book* (IMP/Miller Freeman 1993); *The Gretsch Book* (IMP/Miller Freeman 1996); *The Rickenbacker Book* (IMP/Miller Freeman 1994); *The Ultimate Guitar Book* (DK/Knopf 1991).
Tony Bacon & Barry Moorhouse *The Bass Book* (IMP/Miller Freeman 1995).
David Barry *Street Dreams: American Car Culture 1950s-1980s* (Macdonald Orbis 1988).
British Film Institute *British Television* (Oxford University Press 1994).
Tim Brooks & Earle Marshall *The Complete Directory To Prime Time Network TV Shows 1946-Present* (Ballantine 1979).
Bill Bryson *Made In America* (Secker & Warburg 1994).
Bryan Bunch & Alexander Hellemans *Timetables Of Technology* (Touchstone 1994).
Walter Carter *Gibson: 100 Years Of An American Icon* (General Publishing 1994).
Country Music Foundation *Country: The Music and the Musicians* (Abbeville 1995).
Country Music Magazine *The Complete US Country Music Encyclopedia* (Boxtree 1995).
Anthony DeCurtis et al *The Rolling Stone Illustrated History Of Rock'n'Roll* (Plexus 1992).
A. R. Duchossoir *The Fender Stratocaster* (Mediapresse 1988); *The Fender Telecaster* (Hal Leonard 1991); *Gibson Electrics – The Classic Years* (Hal Leonard 1994).
Tom & Mary Anne Evans *Guitars: Music, History, Construction And Players* (Oxford University Press 1977).
Peter Everett *You'll Never Be 16 Again* (BBC 1986).
George Fullerton *Guitar Legends: The Evolution Of The Guitar From Fender To G&L* (Centerstream 1993).
Chris Gill *Guitar Legends: The Definitive Guide To The World's Greatest Guitar Players* (Studio Editions 1995).
Charlie Gillett *The Sound Of The City* (Souvenir 1996).
Gordon Giltrap & Neville Marten *The Hofner Guitar* (IMP 1993).
John Goldrosen & John Beecher *Remembering Buddy* (GRR/Pavilion 1987).
Hugh Gregory *1000 Great Guitarists* (IMP/Miller Freeman 1994).

George Gruhn & Walter Carter *Gruhn's Guide To Vintage Guitars* (GPI 1991); *Electric Guitars And Basses* (GPI 1994).
Bernard Grun *Timetables Of History* (Touchstone 1991).
Peter Guralnick *Last Train To Memphis: The Rise Of Elvis Presley* (Abacus 1995).
Phil Hardy & Dave Laing *The Faber Companion To 20th-Century Popular Music* (Faber 1990).
David Holloway (ed) *The Daily Telegraph: The Fifties* (Simon & Schuster 1991).
Steve Howe & Tony Bacon *The Steve Howe Guitar Collection* (IMP/Miller Freeman 1994).
Adrian Ingram *The Gibson ES-175* (Music Maker 1994).
John A Jackson *Big Beat Heat: Alan Freed And The Early Years of Rock'n'Roll* (Schirmer 1991).
JTG *Gibson Shipping Totals 1946-1979* (JTG 1992).
Barry Kernfeld (ed) *The New Grove Dictionary Of Jazz* (Macmillan 1994).
Allan Kozinn et al *The Guitar: History, Music, Players* (Quarto 1984).
Colin Larkin (ed) *The Guinness Encyclopedia Of Popular Music* (Guinness 1992).
Jon E. Lewis & Penny Stempel *Cult TV* (Pavilion 1993).
Mark Lewisohn *The Complete Beatles Chronicle* (Pyramid 1992).
Colin MacInnes *England, Half English* (Hogarth 1986).
Dave McAleer *The Book Of Hit Singles* (Carlton 1994); *Hit Parade Heroes: British Beat Before The Beatles* (Hamlyn 1993).
Norman Mongan *The History Of The Guitar In Jazz* (Oak 1983).
John Morrish *The Fender Amp Book* (IMP/Miller Freeman 1995).
Hans Moust *The Guild Guitar Book 1952-1977* (GuitArchives 1995).
Norm N. Nite *Rock Almanac: The First Four Decades Of Rock'n'Roll* (HarperPerennial 1992).
Michael Ochs *Rock Archives* (Doubleday 1984).
Robert Palmer *Deep Blues* (Penguin 1982).
Rittor *60s Bizarre Guitars* (Rittor 1993).
James Sallis *The Guitar Players: One Instrument & Its Masters In American Music* (University of Nebraska Press 1982).

Norbert Schnepel & Helmuth Lemme *Elektro-Gitarren Made In Germany* English translation J P Klink (Musik-Verlag Schnepel-Lemme 1988).
Jay Scott *50s Cool: Kay Guitars* (Seventh String Press 1992).
Mary Alice Shaughnessy *Les Paul: An American Original* (Morrow 1993).
David Shipman *Cinema: The First Hundred Years* (Weidenfeld & Nicholson 1995).
Richard R. Smith *Fender: The Sound Heard Round The World* (Garfish 1995).
Maurice J. Summerfield *The Jazz Guitar: Its Evolution, Players & Personalities Since 1900* (Ashley Mark 1993).
John Tobler *This Day In Rock* (Carlton 1993).
Charles Townsend *San Antonio Rose: The Life & Music Of Bob Wills* (University of Illinois Press 1976).
Paul Trynka (ed) *The Electric Guitar* (Virgin 1993).
Paul Trynka & Val Wilmer *Portait Of The Blues* (Hamlyn 1996).
Thomas A Van Hoose *The Gibson Super 400* (GPI 1991).
John Walker (ed) *Halliwell's Filmgoer's Companion* (HarperCollins 1993).
Tom Wheeler *American Guitars* (HarperPerennial 1990).
Joel Whitburn *Pop Memories 1890-1954* (Record Research 1986).
Forrest White *Fender, The Inside Story* (Miller Freeman 1994).
George R. White *Bo Diddley: Living Legend* (Castle Communications 1995).
Michael Wright *Guitar Stories Volume 1: The Histories Of Cool Guitars* (Vintage Guitar Books 1995).
YMM Player *History Of Electric Guitars* (Player Corporation 1988).

We also found useful various back issues of the following periodicals: *Down Beat* (US); *Guitar Magazine* (UK); *Guitar Player* (US); *Guitarist* (UK); *Making Music* (UK); *Melody Maker* (UK); *Metronome* (US); *The Music Trades* (US); *One Two Testing* (UK); *Vintage Gallery* (US); *Vintage Guitar* (US); *20th Century Guitar* (US).

ACKNOWLEDGEMENTS

OWNERS' CREDITS

Guitars photographed came from the following individuals' collections, and we are most grateful for their help.
The owners are listed here in the alphabetical order of the code used to identify their guitars in the Key To Guitar Photographs below.

AHA Alan Hardtke; **AHO** Adrian Hornbrook; **AL** Adrian Lovegrove; **AR** Alan Rogan; **BM** Bill Marsh; **BW** Bert Weedon; **CB** Clive Brown; **CC** The Chinery Collection; **DB** Dave Brewis; **DE** Duane Eddy; **DG** David Gilmour; **DN** David Noble; **GG** Gruhn Guitars; **GW** Gary Winterflood; **HM** Hiromoto Mihara; **JR** John Reynolds; **KC** Keith Clark (Voltage); **LW** Lew Weston; **MD** Malcolm Draper; **MW** Michael Wright; **PD** Paul Day; **PM** Paul McCartney; **PU** Paul Unkert (The Guitar Guy); **RB** Ron Brown; **RG** Robin Guthrie; **SA** Scot Arch; **SB** Song Bird; **SC** Simon Carlton; **SJ** Scott Jennings (Route 66).

KEY TO GUITAR PHOTOGRAPHS

The following key is designed to identify who owned which guitars when they were photographed. After the relevant page number (*in italic type*) we list: the guitar brand and model (and where necessary other identifier), followed by the owner's initials in **bold type** (see Owners' Credits above). For example, '*8/9*: Epiphone Zephyr Emperor Regent **CC**' means that the Epiphone Zephyr Emperor Regent shown across pages 8 and 9 was owned by The Chinery Collection.

Jacket front: Gretsch 1955 Hollow Body **AHO**; 1959 Stratocaster **SA**; Gibson 1959 Les Paul sunburst **SA**; Gibson 1959 ES-335TDN **SA**; Gibson 1958 Flying V **CC**. *Inside front jacket flap:* Gibson 1953 ES-175D **GG**. *8/9*: Epiphone Zephyr Emperor Regent **CC**. *9/10*: Fender Broadcaster **SA**. *10*: Fender Esquire **DG**. *11/12/13*: Gibson Super 400CES **CC**. *12/13*: Gibson L-5CES **BM**. *13*: D'Angelico Excel **AL**. *14/15*: Fender Telecaster **GG**; Vega Duo-Tron **CC**. *16/17*: Gibson ES-295 **GG**; Gibson Les Paul GG. *18/19*: Les Paul gold-top **CC**; Les Paul gold-top leftie **PM**. *20/21*: Gibson ES-175D **GG**. *22/23*: Guild Stuart **PU**; Gretsch Silver Jet **SA**. *23*: Kay Thin Twin **MW**. *24/25*: Les Paul Junior **DN**. *25*: Guild Stratford **GG**; Les Paul Custom **DN**. *26/27*: sunburst Strat **CC**. *27*: 0001 Strat **DG**. *28/29*: red Strat **SA**. *29*: blond Strat **CC**. *30/31/32*: gold Strat **SA**. *33/34/35*: Gretsch White Falcon **SA**. *34/35*: Gretsch White Penguin **CC**. *36/37*: Stratosphere **PD**. *38/39*: Gretsch Hollow Body **AHO**. *39*: Gretsch Solid Body **LW**. *40/41*: Hofner Club 50 **RB**. *41*: Supro Belmont **CC**. *42/43*: Gibson ES-350T **SA**. *43*: Gibson ES-5 Switchmaster **SA**; Gibson Byrdland **SA**. *44/45*: Danelectro U1 **AHA**; Fender Musicmaster **RG**. *45*: Danelectro U2 **AHA**; Fender Duo-Sonic **RG**. *46/47*: Rickenbacker

Combo 400 **KC**. *48/49*: Guyatone EG-300 **SB**. Teisco J-1 **HM**. *50/51*: Gretsch Country Gent **GG**; Les Paul Custom **CC**. *52/53/54*: Kay Jazz Special **CC**. *53/54*: Harmony Stratotone Newport **MW**; Kay Pro **CC**. *55/56/57*: Les Paul Sunburst **SA**. *58/59*: Les Paul Junior **CB**. *59*: Les Paul TV **SC**. *60/61*: Epiphone Emperor **AR**; Epiphone Crestwood **AR**. *62/63*: Fender Jazzmaster **GG**. *64/65*: Flying V **CC**. *65*: Flying V **GG**. *66/67*: Explorer **CC**; Double 12 **MD**. *67*: Kay Solo King **MW**. *68/69*: ES-335TDN **SA**; ES-335TDN Bigsby **CC**. *69*: ES-335TD **GW**. *70/71*: Guyatone LG-60B **HM**. *71*: Magnatone Mark V **MW**; Magnatone Mark III Deluxe **MW**; Guyatone LG-30 **DB**. *72/73*: Gretsch Country Club Stereo **JR**. *74/75/76*: Rickenbacker 360 **SJ**. *75/76*: Danelectro Long Horn **DE**. *77/78*: Gibson ES-345TDN **SA**; Gibson ES-355TD-SV **DN**. *78/79*: Les Paul Special leftie **SJ**; Les Paul Special **PU**. *80/81*: Hofner Golden Hofner **BW**. *81*: Harmony Stratotone Jupiter **MW**. *82*: Framus Hollywood **PD**. *82/83*: Vega 1200 Stereo **CC**. *83*: Futurama **PD**. *Jacket back flap*: Guyatone LG-30 **DB**. *Jacket back*: Gretsch Country Gent **GG**.

Principal photography was by Miki Slingsby. A small number of additional pictures were taken by Garth Blore, Nigel Bradley, Matthew Chattle, Kazumi Ohkuma, John Peden and Mitch Tobias.

MEMORABILIA

Memorabilia illustrated in this book, including advertising, brochures, catalogs, factory logs, magazines, patents, record sleeves, photographs and tags (in fact anything that isn't a guitar) came from the collections of: Charles Alexander; Scot Arch; Tony Bacon; Ray Butts; Jennifer Cohen; The Chinery Collection; Paul Day; Ross Finley; Gibson Guitar Corp; Karl Erik Hagström; George Martin; Ted McCarty; *The Music Trades*; The National Jazz Archive (Loughton); Ian Purser; Don Randall; Alan Rogan; Steve Soest; Maurice Summerfield; Bert Weedon. We are grateful for their permission to photograph the various items and reproduce them in this book; they were transformed for your visual delight by lensperson Miki Slingsby. Special thanks to Steve Soest for letting out the babies.
We are also grateful to the following for permission to reproduce existing photographs: The British Film Institute (Third Man p10; Girl Can't Help It p14, p47; Rebel p35; Rock Around The Clock p45; Jailhouse Rock p51; Peter Gunn p57); André Duchossoir (McCarty with all-gold Gibson p17); Hiroyuki Noguchi (Guyatone catalogue p49); Redfern's (Muddy Waters p59; Howlin' Wolf p59; Elmore James p61; Gatemouth Brown p63; Guitar Slim p63); Rickenbacker International Corp (girl with guitar p74); Sears Roebuck & Co (catalogues p55/56); Sotheby's London (Holly poster p46; Beatles p83).

Head-and-shoulders illustrations (McCarty p18; Fender p26; Fullerton/Tavares/White p27; Carson p29; Gretsch p33; Matsuki p49; Katz p53; Stathopoulo p61) are by Marïon Appleton.

IN ADDITION to those already named we would like to thank: Charles Alexander; Chet Atkins; Julie Bowie; Harold Bradley; Dave Burrluck (*The Guitar Magazine*); Billy Byrd; Mike Carey (The Chinery Collection); Bill Carson; Walter Carter (Gibson); Christie Carter (Gruhn Guitars); Scott Chinery; Clay; Neil Cope (Giltrap & Cope); Mick Cushing (Type Technique); Vicki Cwiok (Sears Merchandising Group); Kevin Dodd (Type Technique); André Duchossoir; Dan Forte; Grady Gaines; Charlie Gillett; Tommy Goldsmith; George Gruhn; John Hammel (MPL); Brian Jacobs (Rittor); Mikael Jansson; Stan Jay (Mandolin Bros); Paul Johnson (Gruhn Guitars); Ken Jones (National Jazz Archive); Bridget Kinally (British Film Institute); Brian Majeski (*The Music Trades*); George Martin; Steve Maycock (Sotheby's London); Didi Miller (Redfern's); John Morrish; Hans Moust; Mike Newton; Hiroyuki Noguchi (*Guitar Graphic*); Les Paul; John Peden; Bob Pinson (Country Music Foundation); Ronnie Pugh (Country Music Foundation); Don Randall; Rikky Rooksby (Izumi Sato (Rittor); Martin Scott (MPL); Carl Smith; Steve Soest & Amy Soest (Soest Guitar Repair); Barry Spence (Jerry Goldsmith Film Music Society); Sally Stockwell; Maurice Summerfield; Ray Topping (Ace Records); Paul Trynka; Jim Werner; Larry Wexer (Mandolin Bros); Tom Wheeler; Michael Wright.

PRODUCTS of the 1950s involved with this book: Tony Bacon produced in London, England, January 1954 by Pat and Bill; Dave Burrluck produced in Colchester, England, December 1956 by Joan and Jim; Walter Carter produced in Atlanta, Georgia, US, July 1950 by Elizabeth and Walter; Mick Cushing, produced in London, England, May 1956 by Beryl and Henry; Kevin Dodd produced in Gravesend, England, February 1953 by Joyce and Douglas; Tommy Goldsmith produced in Durham, North Carolina, US, February 1952 by Mary and Richard; John Morrish produced in Bristol, England, March 1957 by Zena and Alan; Rikky Rooksby produced in London, England, January 1958 by Dallas and Brian; Larry Wexer produced New York, New York, US, November 1953 by Renée and Martin. Production data on the rest of the team will unfortunately have to wait for *Classic Guitars Of The 1940s* and *Classic Guitars Of The 1960s*.

"The past is a foreign country: they do things differently there." **L. P. Hartley**, 1953.